Lourene —
To a ch
Bless ...

Heb. 11:6

When Faith Matters Most

Marc Cargill

xulon PRESS

Contents

Dedication

This book is dedicated to the people who have most impacted my life with their faith when it mattered most. Without their immeasurable impact on my life, I would not be the person I am today.

First, to my wife, Cheryl, who took a giant leap of faith in marrying me and continued steadfastly in faith as we have faced many times and seasons where faith mattered most. From moving to a small town from her beloved Portland, to following me on the adventure of planting a church in Phoenix, Arizona; or facing the overwhelming challenge of raising children with special needs—she has demonstrated an immovable spirit of faith in her God, her family, and in me. I am and will always be blessed above all men to have her as my partner in life.

To my parents, Jim and Roberta Cargill, who raised me to love God with all my heart, soul, mind, and strength. As pioneers in God's kingdom, they planted three churches and imparted into my sister and I a tenacious spirit of faith and commitment to the Church. I was born again in their church; water baptized in their church; and filled with the Spirit in one of their meetings. The foundation of faith was laid deep in me and I will be eternally grateful to them.

To my sister Michelle, who has always been one of my biggest fans and supporters. Her positive spirit and outlook on life is an inspiration to everyone who knows her. She is truly an example of someone who stands in faith when it matters most.

To my dear friend and mentor in the faith, Pastor Wendell Smith, who has modeled the most balanced message of faith in the Church today. His leadership and influence has helped to establish and shape my spirit of faith and I believe he has introduced the truths of faith, healing, prosperity for a purpose, and apostolic ministry in a fresh way to this generation of leaders. His example of faith in the midst of trial is indescribable and truly exemplary.

To Lighthouse Christian Center, the church I was privileged to plant with my mom and dad—you have been my proving ground and test lab for these truths of faith. You have stood with my family through excruciating tests of faith and we have stood at the base of the mountain of adversity together. Through faith we have overcome these mountains and have proven the principles of faith. I honor you for standing with us in faith when faith mattered most.

Finally, to Hope Church, our wonderful venture of faith in Phoenix, Arizona. To all who have partnered with us, to those who have given up many things to be with us, and for all those who are still coming—Jesus will build His Church and the gates of hell will not prevail against it! You are the fruit of our labor faith and we are forever grateful for your faith in us!

Introduction

Every person has been given a measure of faith. The bible plainly teaches that God implanted in each person this seed of faith. Some people grab a hold of this faith and maximize it to live their life with destiny and powerful purpose! Some marginalize their faith and live in mediocrity. Still others ignore this precious gift of faith and do nothing with it—living far from God and not knowing the great adventure of the life of faith.

No matter where you are in this 'faith spectrum' you will find yourself facing situations or circumstances in life that will test you to the core. Tragedy, testing, problems, decisions, relationships, and many more areas of life demand more than just an educated mind. They require a spirit of faith to not only address them, but to conquer them and emerge from the test victorious!

I have known many people who have tried to handle life's difficulties with only the resources of their education or life experience. Others have sought the advice of counselors and the wisdom of men. But eventually one realizes that no amount of education could prepare them to overcome all of life's challenges. We are just not that smart or experienced. Sooner or later we realize that we must have the involvement of God in our lives to overcome or handle these seasons of need.

This book is a call to everyone to grab on to that faith given to you by God—to increase it and maximize it in your life. The apostle Peter said it well when he wrote, "Dear friends, don't be surprised at the fiery trials you are going through, as if something strange were happening to you." (1 Peter 4:12 NLT) We all will face difficult times and seasons in life. Instead of handling them on our own strength, we must face them with tremendous faith. These times of testing are when Faith Matters Most.

Chapter 1
Fight the Good Fight of Faith

"Fight the good fight of faith, lay hold on eternal life, to which you were also called and have confessed the good confession in the presence of many witnesses."
I Timothy 6:12 (NKJV)

When I was set in as the Senior Pastor of our church, I had no idea of the kind of struggle I was about to engage in. To some, it may seem just an unfortunate string of circumstances, but to me it was a fight of faith. In other words, I had to fight to keep my faith strong and my perspective right.

Labor Day weekend of that year I was playing flag football with some guys from the church and having a blast— acting like I was younger than I really was. Somewhere in the game, I caught a pass and ran up the field. I was making good ground and, hoping to score a touchdown, I put a move on the opponent in front of me that would have made an All-Pro proud. Well almost. As I juked one way and moved the other, my ankle gave a loud "snap" and down I went—the easiest flag pull of the day. Needless to say, I was not only down, I was out. I knew something was pretty wrong with my ankle, but wanting to play the part of tough athlete, I sat on the sidelines weakly cheering my team on and watching the game. The longer I sat there the stronger the throbbing became in my ankle. My wife, Cheryl, did her best to be comforting and finally I said, "We'd better go to the hospital. I think it's pretty serious."

Several hours and a few x-rays later, the doctor confirmed the worst. I had broken my ankle. They put on a cast that reached from the tips of my toes to just below my knee. Then it was the usual "keep this on for six weeks" speech from the doctor. It would not have been so bad except that I would have to wear this crazy thing while preaching in front of my congregation for the next six weeks. And in four weeks there was the official transition of leadership between my predecessor (who happened to be my father) and me. It was supposed to be a glorious event without the curious appendage. And now, it would be cumbersome, uncomfort-able, but more than that—embarrassing.

At the time, Cheryl and I were parents of one child. A boy, who was all I had hoped for—cute, but most important to me, a boy! We were so proud. Just looking into his sleeping face we would imagine him playing sports, or singing in the school choir, or just talking and laughing together about life. But one month after I broke my ankle, we discovered something heartbreaking—our son was deaf.

We had had our suspicions for some time. Yet, I was always in denial. My wife had been doing homemade hearing tests. She had noticed that he never jumped at loud sounds and never woke from sleep because of a loud disturbance. It struck her as odd and so she performed her little tests. She would sneak up behind him and clap her hands loudly. He would just sit there playing, not even noticing or turning to the sound. She told me about it, but being in denial, I was not too convinced of her conclusions. One day when he was sleeping in his crib, my wife got a pan and a large metal spoon. We crept into his room and beat that pan and screamed at the top of our lungs—nothing. My wife burst into tears and I stood there in disbelief.

We later took him to Children's Hospital in Seattle where they tested his hearing. I'll never forget when the audiologist sat down with Cheryl and I and told us our son, who we had hoped to talk with and sing with, was profoundly deaf.

Only two months later, while on our way to my birthday party, our son, who had been sick with a mild fever, suddenly began convulsing in his car seat. We had no idea what was happening and I totally lost control of my emotions and began crying like a baby and calling on the name of the Lord, more in panic than in faith. It was about twenty minutes to the hospital and it was the longest twenty minutes of my life.

Test after test was performed and finally the doctor told us that his fever had spiked and his body had went into a febrile seizure. He told us that they had performed a spinal tap and it appeared that he had spinal meningitis, but that they would have conclusive results in twenty-four to forty-eight hours. So, for the next two days Cheryl and I, and hundreds of our friends and church people, were standing in prayer for a miracle. When the deadline came the doctor called with the news. They had a contaminated sample in the beginning and later testing had proven that he did not have spinal meningitis.

If these things were not enough, my wife discovered a lump in her breast that aroused great concern from her physician. Tests were performed and it was decided that surgery was required to remove the lump. Right about then I was wondering what I had done to bring all these things upon me. What great sin had I committed that deserved this kind of judgment? I know that many people have had an even greater assault on their faith than this, but I was feeling pretty overwhelmed right about then. Not only had I been shocked by all the previous events, but now, the love of my life was in danger. Over the next few weeks I prayed for Cheryl like I had never prayed for her before. I fought for healing and deliverance. I stood on every healing scripture I could find. I confessed and declared my faith in God's power to heal and deliver.

The day of her surgery came. Everything went smoothly and the doctor said the lab would have the results in a few days. "In a few days?!," I thought, as I sat there in the room. "With all the technology there is today, you guys can't place the tissue in some container and do some 'CSI' trick that will reveal everything in an hour? They do it every week on the show?!" Needless to say, my wife and I, and my bad attitude, left the hospital pretty low.

Within a few days we received the news that my wife's tissue had tested benign. Not only were we relieved, but I was thinking, "Whew! At least this is turning out for good." Little did I know that we were going to go through still more adversity. And it would require us to fight the good fight of faith!

It Is A Good Fight

I know what you're thinking. I know because I thought it too. "What could possibly be *good* about this?! What possible good can come from this situation?" Yet in spite of all these questions, the scripture calls it "the good fight of faith." You may be thinking, "Oh yeah? Well, what's so good about it?" I believe there are several reasons why the fight is good.

1. **It is a good fight because God, the Captain of our Salvation, is good.** It's a good fight of faith because God is good. The Captain is good. The Leader of the battle for our side is a good leader. It's a good fight because God has never lost a battle. And if we are following God and He's never lost, and He never will lose, that means that we're going to win the war we're

fighting. He looks out for his troops. He looks out for those who are on His side. He watches over them. He guards them. He helps them. He strengthens them. He is a good God! I think we need to keep remembering and keep confessing the goodness of God in our warfare. When you're in the fight of faith, you need to remember and confess that your God is good. That the One who is leading you in this battle is good. That means it's going to turn out good. It's going to end up good. When it's all said and done it's going to be good. The victory that He's going to lead us into is going to be good—because our Leader is good. He's a good God. The Captain of our Salvation is good. That is one reason why it's a good fight because He is a good God. And we've got to remember that. Think about all the things that you'll learn from the struggle. Why? Because He is good.

2. **It is a good fight because even the things our enemy has meant for evil, God turns to good.** That's what the Bible says. It's taken right out of the scripture that what the enemy intended for evil; what those who would try to steal or kill or destroy, God will

turn it around for good! The Bible story that teaches us this principle is about Joseph, who, after many years, reveals himself to his brothers who betrayed him. They had sold him as a slave. After a remarkable journey of trials and tests, Joseph becomes one of the greatest rulers in the world, second in power only to Pharoah, King of Egypt. When his brothers come from their homeland to Egypt to find relief from famine, they are standing before their brother without realizing it is him. When Joseph finally reveals himself to his brothers, they are greatly afraid for their lives, thinking he will now take his revenge. Instead, Joseph says to them, "Don't be afraid...Don't you see, you planned evil against me, but God used those same plans for my good..." (Genesis 50:20 MESSAGE) That is a testimony to what God does in battle for us. This is what makes our fight a good fight. I realize that we have a nasty devil and that we are facing an enemy who wants to destroy, kill, ruin, and to steal from our lives. The God that we serve is a good God and when the enemy tries to bring evil on us, God will end up turning it for good!

3. **It is a good fight of faith because it will make us stronger.** I was watching a war movie once and there was a part in the film where new recruits arrived at the front lines. Not long after their arrival, a gun went off and they are diving for cover. Meanwhile, the guys that had been on the frontline for a while, the veterans, were not even phased by the gunfire. They were used to it. After awhile their courage had gotten stronger, their strength and their endurance was stronger. The new arrivals had been through boot camp and prepared for battle. Then they *experienced* a battle and they were thinking, "Whoa!! This is serious!" And as they go through the battle they get stronger and stronger. The same thing happens with you. As you serve God and fight battles and win battles, and fight battles, and you might lose a few battles—but you keep on going. God will use the battle to make you stronger. The reason why this fight is good is because you get stronger. You become a stronger Christian, you serve God better, you know the Bible more, you know how to pray better, your faith gets bigger, your faith is stronger, your patience is better, your self-control is different, your long-suffering and your idea

and understanding of who God is and what He can do through your life is totally different than the day when you first signed up for this thing. Why is this a good fight? Because it makes you stronger! Why is it a good fight? Because we can defeat the devil. I don't know about you, but beating the devil makes me really happy!

4. **It is a good fight because we take the spoils of the battle.** I think spoils of the battle can be different things, for example: things the devil has stolen from you. You fight the good fight of faith and you get to take them back. One thing that's really interesting, if you understand warfare and taking back the spoils, it is usually more than what you lost. That's the good thing about spoils. I was watching the news one time and they were interviewing a soldier who was a corporal. He hadn't been in the armed forces for very long, and he'd recently been in Iraq and he had left his family and his nice home. In this story they had shown where he had come from, all these things that he had left in order to go over to another place and fight for freedom. The interviewer asked him, "Are you

really discouraged that you aren't able to be at home with your family?" He replied, "Well, not really." He said, "I miss my family and I miss my country and all of that. But it's not every night you get to sleep in a palace." You see, he was with the headquarters detail. He was in one of Sadaam Hussein's palaces. And he got to sleep in the palace. That's called spoils of war. What has the enemy stolen from you? How has he robbed you? What has he taken? With the help of God you can take back what the enemy has stolen. You can plunder his plans and cancel his ploys. You can take back ground that he has taken from you!! It is not going to be surrendered without a fight, but if we stand strong in faith and fight under the direction of our Commander—we will win! We will conquer! We will take the spoils from our enemy and see restoration in our lives. Now *that* is good!

5. **It is a good fight because, eventually, we possess the gates of our enemies.** The Bible says that part of our inheritance, as the people of God, is that we will possess the gates of our enemies (Genesis 22:17). Gates represent places of influence. They represent

places of power. They represent points of access. And we're able to take the stronghold of the enemy and turn it into a stronghold for God. This is what I call the Kingdom of God advancing. And the good thing about the fight of faith is that when you hang in there and you're not overwhelmed, but you keep going, you will possess the gates of your enemy. This is where God gives you the ability to take what was once a stronghold for the enemy and turn it into a stronghold for God. I've seen people with a spirit of rebellion and stubbornness come to God and that stronghold gets transformed and changed in their life and now they're a sweet, submitted person to the will of God and to God's purpose for their life. But they are the kind of people that never give up. They grab a hold of something and they don't give up for God. That stubbornness that was once unredeemed has been redeemed and changed, and now they have transformed that stronghold of ungodliness into a stronghold of righteousness. What was sinful rebellion now gets transformed and changed, and God makes it into a stronghold of righteousness that won't quit, won't give up, and will hang in there through thick and thin.

They have fought the fight and possessed the gates of their enemies.

This is a good fight! We have a good God. We're going to see God turn what the enemy meant for evil into good. We're going to be stronger. We're going to defeat the devil, take the spoils of the battle and possess the gates of the enemy!

Defining "Fight"

The word "fight" (Greek – *agonizomai*) means *to enter a contest: contend in the gymnastic or Olympic games. To contend with adversaries, fight.* It is also a metaphor used to illustrate what it means to contend or struggle with difficulties and dangers. Finally, it *means to endeavor with strenuous zeal, strive: to obtain something.*

What is unique about this definition is the word "difficulty." This fight is filled with difficulties. They relate to the issues of your own personality and your own life. Difficulties are the things that are *within* you—circumstances and defects in your character and nature that you must deal with. Dangers are the things that are *outside* of you—things that you can't control. They are the designed plans of the enemy to attack your life.

The term 'fight' also means *to endeavor with strenuous zeal, strive: to obtain something. Agonizomai* is where we get the word agonize—to really strive for something so that you might obtain it. This fight that I'm talking about is no walk in the park. It is often agonizing and requires immense effort and hope on our part to endure the battle. There is a lot of "holy sweat" that comes from our lives as we fight this fight of faith.

Ready or Not

This is really important for you to know: we are in a fight. Now I want you to get this: We can't choose whether we are in the fight or not. In this fight there is no such thing as a 'conscientious objector.' The devil has declared war on you whether you are a Christian or not. The enemy has declared war and he wants to steal, kill and destroy. He has declared war and you can't say "But I'm a peace loving Christian. I'm not going to be involved in warfare." Sorry! You're in warfare. It's like some peacenik walking into a warzone saying, "I'm not in this war," and some terrorist pushes a button and blows the guy up. Now that may seem crass or even harsh, but it is so important that we grasp this concept: like it or not you're in the war. We need to make up our mind right now, we are in a battle and we might as well fight.

It must be the way I'm wired, but I am not satisfied with waiting for an attack to come. I would rather be on the offensive instead of the defensive. I don't want to *be attacked.* I want to attack the enemy. I don't want to be overcome. I want to be an overcomer. I don't want to be a victim of the warfare. I want to be a victorious person in the battle! So when it comes to the fight of faith we need to attack! We need to fight!!

The enemy of your soul is going to attack your faith. Even now the devil is attacking you and will continue attacking you. He will attack your faith. He will attack your spouse. He's going to attack your children. He's going to attack your money. He's going to attack your friends, your potential, your mind, your emotions, your spirit, your integrity, your confidence, your hope, and your possessions. And that's the short list. So every one of us need to make a decision in our mind that we're going to obey the scripture here in 1 Timothy 6:12 and fight the good fight of faith!

Fighting To Win:

I've taken the word FIGHT and put it in an acrostic to illustrate five key principles that will help you win this fight of faith.

Fight! Rise up!

Don't be overwhelmed. Stir yourself. Your victory is nearer than you believe. Shake off the weariness of the battle. Shake off the discouragement from the bad reports, the setbacks, and the fears.

F stands for the word "Fight." I know the whole acrostic is fight, but I think it is really important that you understand that this is not time for you to roll over. This isn't time for you say, "I need a break, or I need to run up the white flag. Or I need to have a vacation from the battle." You don't take a vacation from battle. You might take a vacation from your job. You might take vacation from school, but you don't take vacation from fighting the good fight of faith. So I want to encourage you to FIGHT!

You may be overwhelmed! You may have received a bad report! Others of you have been diagnosed. Still more have been experiencing a discouragement or some kind of emotional low place that's going on in your life. Some of you have been dealing with life-long weaknesses in your flesh and you need to fight the good fight. Fight it! Fight that anger problem! Fight that bondage of worry in your life. Fight that spirit of lust that might be in your heart. Fight those things. Don't just say, "Oh I can't help it, I've just been this way!" Oh, you're that way if you give up, but if you fight you can change. You must decide to fight. Don't surrender and say it's all over. You heard the word cancer and said, "Oh no! It's all over!" No! Fight the good fight. Fight that thing. Don't be overwhelmed.

I believe the word "fight" is calling you and to me to stir ourselves up. In ancient times, even the Native Americans, before they prepared themselves for battle, would stay up all night long. Some people would recommend, if you're going to go out to battle the next day, to have a good meal before you go to bed, get a good night's sleep, get a good breakfast before the break of dawn, and then charge the enemy. Be ready. The Native Americans used to do it differently. They would have this great big meal and then they'd stay up all night chanting and dancing. What were they doing? They were stirring themselves up! Getting ready for the battle. They weren't in the tent sleeping. They were ready for battle. And I think that there's a principle that all of us need to learn from. We need to stir ourselves up. Every high school football player knows what I'm talking about. Every basketball player, baseball player, or wrestler understands what I'm talking about. Because in that locker room before you take the field or you take the court, and the coach is done with his pre-game plan and his pep talk, he leaves you alone and later comes back in and says, "All right! We are going to go out there and we are going to win this game!" And everybody then stands up yells, "Yeah!" They start beating on one another's shoulder pads. These guys get so worked up they lose all sense of what's cool. I mean there are eighteen-year-old guys actually reaching out and touching the backsides of other guys around them. They would not do that in any other setting. They don't walk down the hallway doing that! But you get them in a locker room before a football game, "Come on man! Yeah! Let's go! Let's go! Let's go!" Teammates saying, "Hit me again!" You understand what I'm talking about? I'm talking about stirring yourself up. If that's what we do for a game, think about what we should do for the fight of our life! Think about what we should do for the fight of faith! We need to stir ourselves up!!

This is a battle. Your family is in the balance. Your future is in the balance. Your destiny, your character, and much more are in the balance. Your marriage, your children, whatever! It's in the balance! Fight! Shake off the discouragement from the bad report. Shake off the set backs that you've had. Shake off the fears. You might be receiving radiation treatments. You might be receiving chemotherapy. You might be doing some of those things, but don't be afraid! God is with you! Fight!

Insist on victory!

Confess your victory. Declare it! "I'm not going to lose this fight! I'm not going to let the enemy defeat me! I'm not going to let the enemy overwhelm me!" What am I doing? I am confessing with my mouth what I believe in my heart. In Romans 10:8 NKJV it says "'The word is near you, in your mouth and in your heart' (that is the word of faith which we preach)."

I had a good conversation with a friend who had learned a really interesting lesson about thinking differently *combined with* confessing what you are thinking. Many times so many of us say things about ourselves that only reinforce our bad behavior. You do something wrong and you say, "Oh what a jerk! Why did I do that?" That's the wrong thing to think and the wrong thing to say. He said, "You know, it is really important for us to learn to say, "That's not like me." You said something wrong to your wife. You said something bad to your kids or whatever, and you *should* say, "You know, that's not like me" and then respond properly to the situation. This is crucial to our victory because what you believe is what you become. If you believe you're going to be a man of God, that you are like Christ, if you allow yourself to think that and to declare that, things will begin to change. If you reinforce a negative part of your life, you're going to stay in that bad place. But if you reinforce in faith who you are, and what you're going to do, and you declare it out of your mouth, you will change.

The next step my friend recommends is to declare, "I will do better next time." "That's not like me. I'm going to do better next time." What is he saying? He is prophesying to himself. He is prophesying to his future! He is saying, "I'm not that kind of guy; I am better than that. And I'm going to do better next time." He is setting in his heart a way of thinking. And as a man thinks in his heart so is he. It's a principle right out of the Bible.

Since your words have such power, insist on victory. Confess it, believe it, declare it. "My marriage is better than this. We're going to do better." "That's not like us." It is a powerful principle when dealing with your children. There have been times I'd talk with my kids and say something that wasn't right. One time one of my kids was cleaning their room and I went in their room and it was about half done. And I said to them, "That's not like you. You're a hard working, conscientious young man. You can do better." He went in to his room to give it another try. And you know what? The next time I went in to see what he did, it was great! I'm convinced that we get what we believe for. And if all we believe for is the negative and we believe the report of the enemy, that is what we will get. We need to insist on victory. We need to insist this is God's will. That I'm going to be an overcomer! Insist on being the head and not the tail. Insist that you are going to be above and not beneath—that the enemy is going to be crushed under your feet. Insist that you are victorious! You need to insist, confess and believe the word of God. Insist on victory.

Good attitude!

Attitude is everything. This is one of the most difficult principles to practice. One of my mentors in the faith, and someone that I think is probably the best in being an example in this area is Pastor Wendell Smith at the City Church. I mean he tells everybody, and I believe it to be true, "Attitude is everything." If our attitude is wrong, everything will go wrong because attitude is everything.

John Maxwell says that "attitude determines your altitude". The mantra of the Air Force is Aim High. If you want to get there you must have the attitude to go there. And if you want to go to the next level, you've got to have an attitude that is going to help you get to the next level. But if your attitude is bad, or one of self-pity, or you're doing the "woe is me" thing, or that "life stinks", or your attitude is negative, angry, proud, or any number of these things. You will not win this good fight of faith! All of those things are just going to serve to destroy your life in the battle. But if your attitude is good, humble, meek, one of strength and glory unto the Lord, if your attitude is one that is modeling the fruit of the spirit, your good attitude will determine the outcome of the battle.

There's a film about a Scottish warrior who is leading Scotland in the struggle for freedom. All of his men on the battle line are standing there thinking, "We're all going to get killed today." He rides up on his horse and he says to his men, "Today, we are going to fight a battle." And you can just see the look on their faces, "We're going to fight all right. We're going to die right here!" They saw all the English knights and armies just across the field—poised to destroy them. The leader's attitude was, "I've won this thing and no one has even drawn a sword yet and we're going to win!" That was his attitude. And you know what? The longer he talked, that attitude began to be caught by the other warriors. Finally at the end of his inspiring speech, he starts riding off towards the English lines and one of the men looks at him and asks, "What are you doing?" and he says, "I'm going to pick a fight." Because of that winning attitude, the Scots won the day.

Attitude is a very powerful thing. And it will determine your success in the battle. I've got to tell you though, out of all the things I'm sharing with you, this is probably the hardest one to do.

I had a personal moment with a friend who has been diagnosed with cancer and is fighting the good fight of faith. We are believing for his complete and total healing. But he was just sharing with me that he has bad days. It just happens. Everyone has days when you don't feel very victorious. Having a good attitude is not easy. It is hard. But my friend doesn't allow himself to stay in a wrong attitude. He embraces and puts on the attitude of faith. As a result, he has outlived every doctor's prediction of death. I believe his attitude has made a difference. Maybe your struggle has to do with victory in your finances. You just got another bounced check notice in the mail or you had a big fight with your spouse and you're thinking, "It's just like we aren't making any headway here!" Guard your attitude. It will be hard, and it will be difficult. But keep a good attitude.

Hallelujah your way to victory!

What does the word hallelujah mean? It means praise the Lord. "Praise the Lord" your way to victory. There is a story in the Bible where God's people were facing an enemy and they were severely outnumbered. But do you know what God tells them to do? He tells them to put the worship band out in front of the army and He says, "I want you to march towards the valley where you're going to meet your enemies for battle. This is what I want you to do. I want you to sing this song over and over again: "'For the Lord is good and his mercy endures forever.'" As incredible as it seems, they got all the musicians out in front and they did exactly what God told them to do. And when they got to the valley, all of their enemies were dead. They had won a great victory! How did it happen? The Bible says God sent angels to fight for His people. They didn't have to draw one sword out of its sheath. All they had to do was worship God.

I think this is a very powerful principle. If we want to fight the good fight of faith, get your "hallelujah" on. Put on your favorite worship CD or come to church and just throw yourself into it. In spite of all the junk and in spite of all the garbage that is going on just say, "You know what? I'm going to hallelujah my way out of this thing! I'm going to hallelujah my way to victory. I'm going to say, "The Lord is good and His mercy endures forever!" And you watch – God will show up!

The thing I love to do more than anything else is just 'hallelujah' my way. If I do that, man, I feel the burden just lift. I feel peace come into my spirit. I feel faith rise in my heart. There is something about when I worship God—I connect with Him and when I connect with Him, fireworks just start going off in my spirit. At that point, I know that I can do anything.

The Psalms tell us, "Magnify the Lord and let us exalt His name together." What does the word 'magnify' mean? To make something big. You use a magnifying glass and it makes things bigger. The point is that if you make God big, all this other stuff becomes irrelevant. Small. You really get some perspective. Big God, little problem. Big God, little devil. Magnify God. Worship your way out of worry! Praise your way out of the problem! Hallelujah your way to victory! It may sound ridiculous—but if you do it, God will show up and do the miraculous!

Together is required!

The scripture tells us "It is not good for man to be alone." (Genesis 2:18) And elsewhere it even says, "Woe to him who is alone…though one may be overpowered, two can withstand him, and a threefold cord is not easily broken." (Ecclesiastes 4:10-12)

What's the principle there? You don't want to ever fight a battle by yourself. You want to have togetherness with other people. But here's the problem. Most people that I know when they get attacked, and they go through a very trying time in their life, their tendency is to withdraw. Our tendency is to enclose ourselves. Our tendency is to get back away in the darkness of the cave and just kind of stay there. And we can't do that. Together is required. The Bible says that as you fight the good fight, the more people you have agreeing with you and fighting alongside you the more enemies you will destroy.

I want to encourage you, when you are going through a fight of faith, especially when the battle really gets hot and you are feeling really overwhelmed, that is not the time to skip church. That is not the time to be absent from your small group. That is not the time to stay away from the youth meeting. That is not the time to skip the ladies' retreat. That is not the time to say, "Aw, I don't think I should go to the men's seminar." That is when you need to be involved the most. It is when you need to not only pay for your way, but also pay for someone else's way to go with you.

Together is required. And if you want to see an over-coming spirit come into your life, have someone there who knows how to overcome and stand with you. Let them be there with you and let their encouragement rub off on you.

I've experienced times when I wanted to give up and I wanted to quit. You know what I did? I got around people who knew what it meant to go through those times, but never did quit. And they understood my emotion, but they said, "You know that God is with you. Let's just pray." And they would put their arm around me. I may cry, I may be frus-trated or whatever, but when we're done, I know I'm going to make it. I know I'm going to be victorious.

Fight the good fight of faith! As you contend for your victory, remember these five things:

Fight! Have a fighting spirit that causes you to fiercely contend for breakthrough.

Insist on victory and don't settle for anything less.

Good attitude is essential because it impacts how you handle emotions and difficulties.

Hallelujah your way to victory because God will champion those who praise Him.

Together is always required because your victory will never be achieved alone.

Chapter 2
Faith for Healing

"Jesus said to him, "If you can believe, all things are pos-
sible to him who believes.""
Mark 9:23 NKJV

Okay, I know we live in the 21st century. There's a
pill for this and a procedure for that, and just about
every time we watch television there's an ad for some
medicinal potion to help you with your ills. Now, I want to
be clear. I have no problem with modern medicine or the
benefits of doctors, hospitals or treatment for sickness and
disease. In fact, I heartily endorse seeking the aid of physicians and medical personnel to help in the treatment of physical or mental health challenges. However, I have watched
as people run first to the healing power of medicine instead

of to the healing Hand of our good and great God—the Lord Who Heals!

I would like to challenge you to say, "I am going to believe God for some healings and some miracles." All right? Would you do that with me? Right now just make up your mind. "I'm going to use my faith today and maybe use my faith in a way I've never used my faith before." Believe God for some miracles and healings!

The Gospels describe the beginning of Jesus' ministry as powerful and miraculous. Jesus ministered healing and deliverance to many people.

*Matthew 4:23-24, "And Jesus went about all Galilee, teaching in their synagogues, preaching the gospel of the kingdom, and healing all kinds of sickness and all kinds of disease among the people. Then His fame went throughout all Syria; and they brought to Him all sick people who were afflicted with various diseases and torments, and those who were demon-possessed, epileptics, and paralytics; **and He healed them**."* (emphasis mine)

Mark 1:32-34 "At evening, when the sun had set, they brought to Him all who were sick and those who were demon-

possessed. And the whole city was gathered together at the door. Then **He healed many** *who were sick with various diseases, and cast out many demons; and He did not allow the demons to speak, because they knew Him."* (emphasis mine)

Luke 4:40 "When the sun was setting, all those who had any that were sick with various diseases brought them to Him; and **He laid His hands on every one of them and healed them**.*"* (emphasis mine)

Jesus' disciples continue this ministry of healing in the book of Acts. Peter is preaching a message and he describes, as an eye-witness, the great miracles that Jesus performed. In Acts 10:38, he reminds them about *"how God anointed Jesus of Nazareth with the Holy Spirit and with power, who went about doing good and* **healing all** *who were oppressed by the devil, for God was with Him."* (emphasis mine)

Do you believe God is with you? Do you believe you have anointing? Do you believe you have the Holy Spirit in your life? If you are a believer you have the same Holy Spirit Peter had! You have the same Holy Spirit Jesus had on His life! The same Holy Spirit that came on Jesus and empowered Him to do the things He did is on you! The same presence of Christ is in you right now and God wants to minister to us and through us so we may minister His healing to people. God wants to heal people today. There is probably someone you know who is sick, infirmed, or ill. They are under attack of disease, infirmity, sickness or some kind of physical problem, and you can stand in behalf of those who are sick and see them healed.

Matthew 17:14-18 tells a powerful story of a boy who was healed because someone stood on his behalf for healing.

"And when they had come to the multitude, a man came to Him, kneeling down to Him and saying," Lord, have mercy on my son, for he is an epileptic and suffers severely; for he often falls into the fire and often into the water. So I brought him to Your disciples, but they could not cure him." Then Jesus answered and said, "O faithless and perverse generation, how long shall I be with you? How long shall I bear with you? Bring him here to Me." And Jesus rebuked the demon, and it came out of him; and the child was cured from that very hour."

I want you to notice how this man came and stood on behalf of the one that was sick and asked Jesus to heal him. If this man had not gone to the One Who Heals, there would have been no miracle. But because someone was willing to intercede and come to Christ for healing, there was deliverance and healing for that young man. Can you imagine the gratefulness of that son for what his father did? Can you hear him telling his father, "Thanks dad. Thank you for believing. Thank you for standing for my healing."

There is also a story of a Roman soldier who came to Jesus on behalf of one of his servants who was very sick. The soldier said unto Jesus "I have a servant at home who is very, very ill. Would you please heal him?" And Jesus said to him, "I will come to him and heal him." The soldier said to Jesus, "No, you don't even have to come. All you need to do is to say the word. Say the word and I know my servant will be healed." Jesus was amazed at this man's faith and spoke the word of healing and the soldier's servant was healed that very hour!!

I believe that as you stand on behalf of other people who are ill or sick, God will use you and your faith, as a point of contact, to send a word and heal that person and make them whole.

Why Does God Want To Heal?

Why does God want to heal us? Is it just a fairy tale or bible story that is limited to bible times and bible characters? Does God want to heal anyone today?

God does want to heal. Consider these four reasons why God wants to heal:

1. **Because it is His nature**. What does the Bible say that God is? God is love, right? And how many loving, caring, compassionate people do you know who, in a heart beat, if they had the power to heal their loved one, friend or neighbor—they would do it! Or let's think about how the Bible says, "The Lord is good and His mercy endures forever." It is *who He is*. He is good. He is a good God. What good doctor—what good physician would not want to see you whole? Would he not want to see you well? I went to see a really good doctor and he said, "I want you to be whole. I'm in the business of putting myself out of business. I don't want the world filled with sick people. I want them whole." God is good. He is the Good and Great Physician. It is because He is good. It is His nature. He *wants* to heal people.

Too many people can get all caught up in the reasoning of the mind about why they're sick. "Okay," they say, "If God is so good, why is there all this disease in the world? Why is there all this sickness in the world?" I actually went through all the stories in the gospels and read every story where Jesus healed someone. One of these miracle stories is about a man who was deaf. And the Bible says that the people who were standing around were saying, "Who has sinned that this man would be deaf?" and Jesus said, "Neither he nor his parents have sinned, but that the glory of God might be revealed has this come upon him." Think about that statement: "That the Glory of God might be revealed." I believe people are sick for a multitude of reasons. But God is not one of them. I also believe that God can take it as an opportunity to show His glory. So when you start getting caught up in why sickness and disease are in the world, think about it this way: all of these things are opportunities for God's glory to show up. It's His nature. Why does he heal? Because He's good. Because He loves you. Because He wants to work things out for good in your life. It's His nature to heal you.

2. It is His Name. One of the names of God in the ancient Hebrew language is *Jehovah Rophe* which is translated "The Lord Who Heals." Healing is His name.

The Bible tells a story of when the people of Israel came to a stream and the water of the stream was so bitter they could not drink it. And if they were to drink it, it would have made them sick. They had traveled a great distance in the desert and were very thirsty. There was a source of water right in front of them, but they couldn't drink it. And so God spoke to Moses, "I want you to take a tree and cut it down and throw it into the water." The tree represents the cross or the sacrifice of Christ. Jesus died on the tree (the Cross) that we might have healing. This tree was cut down and thrown into the waters which were totally healed, the bitterness was gone, and the people were able to drink. Then God declares, *"I will put none of the diseases on you which I have brought on the Egyptians. For I am the LORD who heals you."* (Exodus 15:26)

God was declaring, "I not only have the power to heal the stream, but I have the power to heal you."

He says, "I am Jehovah Rophe, I am the Lord who heals. That is My name."

Most people feel strongly about their name. It stands for reputation, honor, and integrity. A name is a description of who someone is, what they can do, and the character associated with that person. How many of you believe your name is kind of important? The dignity, the respect, the honor and the legacy of your name is important. When someone says your name people should think "They are such a wonderful person." The Lord says, "This is My Name. I am the Lord Who Heals You!" And let me tell you, He wants to live up to His Name!

3. **Because it is His Will.** Lots of people struggle with this statement. So many people battle with this truth. All you have to do is read stories of Jesus healing people. Do you know how many times people came to Jesus and said, "If you are willing would you heal me?" It happened over and over again. And you know what Jesus' response was to them? These were His words: "I am willing. Be healed. I am willing."

Is God willing to heal people? Yes He is. He is willing. It is His will. In Matthew 8 a leper came to Jesus and said, "Lord if you're willing, heal me." Leprosy in Bible times was like the worst diseases today. You could probably name several diseases that may qualify as the top three worst diseases you could have. Maybe cancer or AIDS or some horrible plague you could name. Leprosy was like that.

Another curse of being a leper was they were outcasts. They weren't even allowed to be around other people. They were often quarantined and ostracized from other healthy people. I've been to leper colonies before. I've laid my hands on lepers and prayed for them. I know what it is to see the effects of leprosy first hand. It's a horrible, disfiguring disease. Yet, in spite of the condition of this man, Jesus said, "I am willing. Be cleansed." The Bible says that man was healed that very hour.

As you read the Gospels, is there any record of someone coming to Him for healing and He turned them down? The only situation that may come close was the Canaanite woman who came to Jesus for her demon-possessed daughter (Matthew 15). But even after His hesitation, Jesus healed the little girl. There is no place in the Gospels where Jesus refused to heal someone. He then commands us, His disciples, to go and pray for the sick. Why would He tell us to do that if it was not His will to heal people? Healing, health and wholeness *is* His will. He is willing! Be healed!

4. **Healing is part our inheritance.** The healing power of God is our inheritance. We as believers are also the children of God. We are sons and daughters of faith. We have faith in Christ and so we are in the family of God. He is our Father, we are His children and as such we have an inheritance that is ours.

> Ephesians 1:3 *"Blessed be the God and Father of our Lord Jesus Christ, who has blessed us with every spiritual blessing in the heavenly places in Christ."*

When I read the phrase, "every spiritual blessing," I know that healing is in there. Read the following passage from Ephesians and pay attention to the blessings listed.

Ephesians 1:4-9 *"just as <u>He chose us</u> in Him before the foundation of the world, that we should be holy and without blame before Him in love, having pre-destined us to <u>adoption as sons</u> by Jesus Christ to Himself, according to the <u>good pleasure</u> of <u>His will</u>, to the praise of the glory of <u>His grace</u>, by which He made us <u>accepted</u> in the Beloved. In Him we have <u>redemption</u> through His blood, the <u>forgiveness of sins</u>, according to the <u>riches of His grace</u> which He made to abound toward us in all <u>wisdom</u> and <u>prudence, having made known to us the mystery of His will</u>, according to <u>His good pleasure</u> which He <u>purposed</u> in Himself,"*

Think about these benefits that are ours through faith:

- His good pleasure
- His will
- His grace
- His acceptance
- Redemption

- Forgiveness of sins
- The riches of His grace
- Wisdom
- Prudence
- Purpose

Ephesians 1:11 *"In Him also we have obtained an inheritance, being predestined according to the purpose of Him who works all things according to the counsel of His will, that we who first trusted in Christ should be to the praise of His glory. In Him you also trusted, after you heard the word of truth, the gospel of your salvation; in whom also, having believed, you were sealed with the Holy Spirit of promise, who is the guarantee of our inheritance until the redemption of the purchased possession, to the praise of His glory."*

And later, in verse 17, *"that the God of our Lord Jesus Christ, the Father of glory, may give to you the spirit of wisdom and revelation in the knowledge of Him, the eyes of your understanding being enlightened; that you may know what is the hope of His calling, what are the riches of the glory of His inheritance in the saints, and what is the exceeding greatness of His power toward us who believe, according to the working of His mighty power."*

Now notice the example He gives to show His power in verse 20: *"which He worked in Christ when He raised Him from the dead and seated Him at His right hand in the heavenly places."*

These scriptures speak of the power of God and as an example of His power God uses the resurrection of Christ. I would say that is some serious healing right there. Resurrection is the ultimate healing. When death has come and had its victory over your life and Jesus raises you to life again—that is the ultimate healing. Our healing is part of our inheritance. We have read that Christ has provided us an inheritance through His death on the cross and His resurrection from the dead. The prophet Isaiah declared, "By His stripes we are healed." (Isaiah 53:5) Healing is our inheritance!

I heard of a woman and her husband who were on vacation. They were having such a wonderful time, when suddenly, he dropped to the ground with a heart attack. As her husband lay on the ground gripping his chest she called 9-1-1. The ambulance came and took her husband to the hospital. Being believers, they knew that he would go to heaven if he died, but she prayed that God would save him. She prayed all the way to the hospital, but he died en route. As she was faced with the grim reality of his death, the woman began to pray for life to return to his body! She stood outside the Emergency Room while every effort was made to resuscitate her husband. For minutes they tried to revive him, but to no avail. They called the time of death and the emergency physicians and nurses left while an attendant wheeled out his body and placed it in another room. The woman went into that room and she called out to God. She prayed, "God I'm crying out to you! Would you raise my husband from the dead? Raise him up with the Spirit of Life!" An hour passes, and she continued praying, "Oh God, just touch my husband. Raise his body up from this bed." Two hours went by and still she continued praying and praying, pressing in. Three hours went by and after three hours of desperate intercession, she felt the powerful presence of God as it entered the room. All of a sudden, she heard a gust of wind—a 'whoosh' that came into the room. The man's spirit came back into his body! He opened his eyes and sat up in bed—perfectly and totally whole!!

I was ministering at a church in Japan and there was a man present at the meeting who had a severe case of insomnia. He was not able to sleep for days and he came to the meeting and we were praying for healing that night. When I saw this man he looked like he had been hit by a truck. I mean he just looked horrible. He was all bent over with the fatigue and the stress. It was obvious something was wrong with him as a result of his lack of sleep. His face was gaunt, his eyes were bloodshot and he was about ready to fall over from exhaustion, but he could not go to sleep. We prayed for this man and the power of God came on him and he just began lifting his hands and praying and worshiping God, and I could tell the Holy Spirit was doing something in his body. The next day he was at the church service, but he looked so different that I almost did not recognize him. His eyes were bright, the gauntness of his face was gone, and his body was straight. He even seemed taller as a result of the change in posture. The church leaders came up to me and said, "You must see this man."

Through the interpreter I found out that after the service he went home and as soon as he got home he laid down on his bed and said, "I thank you Lord that I am going to sleep right now and I am healed!" He fell right to sleep and he awoke just in time to catch the train and come to church the next morning. He had slept all night long and was rested the next day. I began pondering this later as I was thinking about this miracle. This man didn't have just one night's sleep. Something happened in his body as if he had gotten three or four nights worth of sleep in one night. What a powerful miracle!

On a trip to India we ministered in a church and a lady had come to the service, but she was not able to walk. They actually carried her into the meeting. They sat her down and we began to sing, worshiping God, praising the Lord and enjoying what God was doing among those precious people. After the preaching of the word we were praying and I felt a spiritual anointing for healing the sick. As we began praying for people they brought this lame woman for prayer. They had a prayer mat that she sat on and they pulled it up to where we were praying. So we just began praying over her and speaking the word of the Lord over her life—that she would be healed, and that she would walk, and that strength would come into her legs. She had not walked since she was six years old. As we were praying, I heard the voice of the Spirit speak to me and say "I want you to take her hand and pull her to her feet." I wish I could say acted immediately and with great faith. The truth is, I stood there wrestling with the direction I had received. Then something burst into my spirit: *If you do the ridiculous, God will do the miraculous*! If you do the ridiculous it releases, because it is an act of faith, the miraculous. I mean it is ridiculous to throw your leg over a boat and expect to walk on water, but it happened. It's ridiculous to spit in dirt, make some mud out of your spit, wipe it on a blind man's eyes and then say I want you to go wash in the pool and think that he's going to be healed from his blindness. He's going to go, "Ow! I got something in my eye, thanks a lot!" The Spirit would not leave me alone with this, but continued to speak to me. "Take her hand and pick her up," so I went over to her and I took her hand and I said, "In the name of Jesus, rise to your feet." And I began to pull her up and she rose, but a little unsteady. Strength was there in her body as she began to stand up. I took her by the elbows to help steady her, and over the course of about thirty minutes, I was leading her by the hand around the room and she walked around that church building!

I want to tell you these stories because you read them in the Bible, but you ask, "Does God really do that in real life today? Does He really do it?" I answer boldly, "Yes He does!!" I've *seen* Him heal people. I know it works. I *know* He heals people.

There are those who pray to be healed and they don't get healed. I can't explain that and I will not even try to explain it. I leave that up to God and when we get to heaven we will have all eternity for Him explain that to us. Somehow I have a feeling you're not going to care when you get there. But may I challenge your thinking here. The bible clearly tells us that God wants everyone to be saved. He is "not willing that any should perish, but that all come to repentance." (2 Peter 3:9) And elsewhere, it says that God "desires all men to be saved and come to the knowledge of the truth." (1 Timothy 2:4) And even though it is God's will for everyone to be saved, not everyone is saved! So do we stop preaching the gospel? Do we stop telling the world about Jesus? Certainly not! Even though everyone we pray for may not get healed, we pray for them and pray in faith believing for their healing. If they are healed— glory to God! If they are not, we trust God and continue to pray for healing!

The truth is, we have an inheritance of healing. The same Holy Spirit that raised Christ Jesus from the dead lives in you! Ephesians says we have this inheritance of resurrection power. In fact, it uses the word inheritance *three times*. The bible says that by the power of the Holy Spirit, God raised Jesus from the dead, and He is referring to the same Holy Power that works in you and me. I believe that the same Spirit that raised Jesus from the dead is the same Holy Spirit that heals people! He can heal your sick body, your friend's body, your neighbor's body, your brother and sister in Christ or whoever you want to stand in for today. God heals people!

The Good News

As I was thinking about healing I felt stirred to read through the gospels about Jesus healing people. I was struck by the responses Jesus gave to people when they came to Him and asked for healing. Take a moment to look at these statements—words that Jesus said to the sick. When they came to be healed they wanted him to touch them, wanted Him to heal them. These are the words Jesus spoke to them when they came to ask for their healing.

To the leper - "I am willing, be cleansed."

To the Centurion whose servant was home sick—"I will come and heal him." And the Centurion says, "No you don't have to come, just say the word and I know my servant will be healed." And Jesus says this, "Go your way. As you have believed, so let it be done for you."

To the paralytic who was lowered through the roof by his friends—"Son, be of good cheer, your sins are forgiven you." If your sins are forgiven that's the greatest miracle. Being healed, that's just the icing. The cake is that your sins are forgiven. "Your sins are forgiven you. Arise!

Take up your bed and go to your house." And for the first time in his life, he walked home!!

The woman with an incurable flow of blood — "Be of good cheer, daughter. Your faith has made you well. Go in peace and be healed of your affliction."

Two blind men — "Do you believe that I am able to do this? According to your faith let it be to you."

A Canaanite woman whose daughter was severely sick — "Oh woman, great is your faith. Let it be to you as you desire."

Jairus, ruler of the synagogue whose daughter was sick and later had died — "Do not be afraid, only believe." How many of you have been in a situation where great fear comes in as the diagnosis is given or the battle and the struggle against the disease is tough and you become afraid? Do you struggle with the fear of dying? Maybe you become afraid of sickness or of being alone. Or maybe you become afraid for your family who may be alone after you die or of some other tragedy. The word of God to you today is "Do not be afraid. Only believe."

Twelve-year-old girl who had died — "Little girl I say to you, arise." And she did. She came back to life!

One who was deaf and mute — Jesus said to his mouth and his ears, "Be open," and they were!

A young man who had died — "Young man I say to you, arise." And he arose from the dead!

A woman who had had a spirit of infirmity for eighteen years and was all bent over — "Woman you are loosed from your infirmity," and she was healed immediately!

Ten lepers — "Arise and go your way. Your faith has made you well."

A nobleman's son on the very verge of death — "Go your way, your son lives."

A man with an infirmity of 38 years — "Do you want to be made well? Rise, take up your bed and walk." Jesus asked this man, "Do you want to be made well?" I think there are some people that really don't want to be made well. You may say, "Now that is a little harsh! That can't be right." But it's true. You see, they get so much attention while being sick—people waiting on them and they get all this care and attention. All the focus is on them. They like all the attention and if they were whole and healed they wouldn't get all those things. I believe that sometimes people don't get healed because they would rather stay sick and get all of that attention. This is an issue of their soul, not an issue of their body. Jesus can heal them, but their soul is not right. Do you want to be made well? "Rise and take up your bed and walk."

A sister whose brother was sick — "This sickness is not unto death, but for the glory of God, that the Son of God may be glorified through it."

Lazarus who had died — "Lazarus come forth." And Lazarus came out of that tomb!

A blind man — "What do you want me to do for you? Go your way, your faith has made you well." I just hear the voice of Jesus saying to people today, "What do you want me to do for you?"

Important Keys For Your Healing

1. **Wisdom and good stewardship of your body**. If you're not getting sleep and you're treating your body poorly, I think it is almost a joke to come and say, "Lord heal me in my body. Heal my sicknesses." We need to be wise stewards of our body. 1 Corinthians 6:19-20. *"Or do you not know that your body is the temple of the Holy Spirit who is in you, whom you have from God, and you are not your own? For you were bought at a price; therefore glorify God in your body and in your spirit, which are God's."* Some of you are workaholics and the best spiritual advice I could give you is: take a day off! Take a day off or you're going to die really, really young. Some of you need to take a vacation. Some of you need to change your diet. Stop drinking so much soda! Others of you need to get more rest. Maybe you need to exercise

more. If we expect to live in health and be in health
and prosper even as our soul prospers, let's take care
of our body.

2. **You need a spirit of faith**. You just read all of those
things Jesus said to those seeking a miracle. There was
a phrase used time and again by Jesus. Did you catch
it? A spirit of faith is an absolute necessity if you're
going to get healed. You must have faith. You've
got to believe God is able to do it. Isn't that what
Jesus said to the man? "Do you believe I am able to
do this?" A spirit of faith. We need to believe God is
able to heal. We must believe that as we pray to Him,
He's going to answer our prayers for healing.

3. **Gifts of healings**. God has given gifts of healings
to the body of Christ. I think it's interesting because
the word 'gifts' in 1 Corinthians 12 is plural. And the
word 'healings' is plural. 'Gifts of healings'. I believe
there are graces or anointings that God gives people
for certain kinds of sicknesses. I've prayed for several couples who were unable to have children and
they have conceived. There is a person in our church

because of the word of the Lord and a miracle. Nicole is the daughter of Ed and Barb Johnson. She is in our church and alive today as a result of a miracle from God. That's pretty amazing if you can actually see somebody and they are alive and they exist because of a miracle. They were created. They were born because of the creative miracle of God. That's just amazing. You can see them every week and say, "There's a miracle! There's a miracle!"

Marilyn Hickey has said she has a unique anointing for healing of warts and goiters and tumors. When asked about it she says, "I don't know...I pray for them and they just get healed immediately." Some of us have gifts of healings for different things and I say whatever it is, if it works, go for it! If every back you pray for gets healed, man I'd start praying for every hurting back I could find!!

4. **The anointing of oil and prayer of the elders.** James 5:14-15 *"Is anyone among you sick? Let him call for the elders of the church, and let them pray over him, anointing him with oil in the name of the Lord. And the prayer of faith will save the sick, and the Lord will*

raise him up. And if he has committed sins, he will be forgiven". Over the years we have followed this principle in our church and it is amazing to see the miracles and healings God has performed!

5. **The prayer of agreement.** Jesus taught us in Matthew 18:19 *"Again I say to you that if two of you agree on earth concerning anything that they ask, it will be done for them by My Father in heaven."* And the key principle here is agreement. I think that if you stand in agreement to believe for healings you are going to see them. If you are facing a diagnosis or some physical problem, find someone to stand in agreement with you in prayers of faith for healing. There is power in agreement. The negative side of this principle is true as well. You can find someone to agree with you for sickness too. I have visited the sick only to hear their spouse say something like, "Your uncle Charlie had that diabetes too and look what happened to him. Lost his foot to that disease. Aunt Thelma agrees with me that it could happen to you too!" That's not the kind of agreement you need!! Have someone agree in faith for your healing!

6. The Word of God. Remember the Roman Centurion who came to Jesus? He had a servant who was sick and he said, "all you need to do is <u>speak the word</u> and I know my servant will be healed." And Jesus said, "I haven't found such great faith in all of Israel." Jesus knew, "All I have to do is say the Word. I don't have to be there, all I have to do is say the Word." Psalm 107:20. *"You sent Your word and healed them."* I believe it works like this: If someone is dealing with cancer, and they're not here, we're going to send a word of healing to heal that cancer. When we send a word of healing, in the Spirit, it will be like an arrow sent from the bow of faith and we're going pray that 'arrow of healing' all the way there and we're going to see God touch those people. We're going to send a word of healing and we're going to say "Cancer! Be healed in Jesus' Name. Raise that person up off that sick bed and let them be completely whole." You can send that sick person words of healing. They can be sent across the Atlantic Ocean. They can be sent across the Pacific Ocean. They can be sent on the other side of the equator. They can be sent to the remotest part of the world and the Word of God that you prayed to a person gets there and can heal them!

7. **The atmosphere for healing**. Luke 5:17 *"Now it happened on a certain day, as He was teaching, that there were Pharisees and teachers of the law sitting by, who had come out of every town of Galilee, Judea, and Jerusalem. And <u>the power of the Lord was present to heal them</u>."* It was as though God's healing presence settled right down upon those present, creating an atmosphere of healing, and Jesus began healing people. I believe there is an atmosphere of faith here today. Right here in this place where you are reading this book, there is an atmosphere of healing. I believe God wants to heal. I believe there is a rain of healing that God wants to rain down on us.

You may be reading this book and the Holy Spirit has begun to minister to you. The scriptures have given birth to faith and you have begun to believe for healing. I believe that many of you reading this will experience the presence of God enter the room where you are sitting and the Spirit of life and healing will begin ministering to you.

There is a popular gospel song recorded by Michael W. Smith entitled, *Healing Rain.* I believe it is a prophetic song—a song describing the cloud of God's presence and the healing rain that falls upon people. God is pouring out His healing rain upon you and all around the world. He is healing the infirmed, the sick, and the dying. He is healing the wounded and broken-hearted! It is our inheritance! It is His promise! Be healed in the name of Jesus Christ!!

Some of you have received a negative report. A doctor has given you his diagnosis and it is not good. Fear has gripped your heart. You've believed their report and you are formulating a course of action. The prophet Isaiah asked, "Who has believed our report?" (Isaiah 53:1) What is *our report?* Our report is God's Word!! Our report is God heals! Our report is God is greater than any sickness, more powerful than any disease, stronger than any diagnosis! Take what faith you have and aim it at that sickness! Boldly pray and declare God's healing power over your life. Maybe it's your spouse or your child or grandchild. It might be a friend or co-worker. Step up with faith and contend for healing and miracles! It's easy to roll over and give in. But let's not do easy! Rise up with faith and face that sickness head on. You have an inheritance for this healing! Healing is God's Name!

Use your faith and give God a chance to live up to His name!! Use your faith! When we are staring a disease or sickness in the eye—it's one of the times when faith matters most!

Chapter 3
Faith For Testing

"Now when He got into a boat, His disciples followed Him. And suddenly a great tempest arose on the sea, so that the boat was covered with the waves. But He was asleep. Then His disciples came to Him and awoke Him, saying, "Lord, save us! We are perishing!" But He said to them, "Why are you fearful, O you of little faith?" Then He arose and rebuked the winds and the sea, and there was a great calm."
Matthew 8:23-26 NKJV

The journey of faith has, for all of us, tests that are given or allowed by God to help us in our maturity and growth. The disciples were given just such a test after Jesus' amazing Sermon on the Mount. When Jesus finished teaching the multitude, He gave instructions to the disciples to get into the boat for they were going to the other side of the lake. During the crossing, a great storm suddenly arose and the disciples began to panic. Thinking they were going to die, they cried out to Jesus who was sleeping in the boat during all the commotion! He stood up in the boat and commanded the wind and the waves to be still—and to the disciples amazement it happened just as He commanded! Jesus then looked at His disciples and rebuked them for having little faith.

Some have wondered why Jesus rebuked them. It certainly seems reasonable for them to be greatly afraid and to cry out for their lives. However, I believe Jesus was testing their faith. The Master had given direction – cross over to the other side. The disciples were tested to see if they believed that they would get there, even when confronted with a storm. You see, when God gives an order, it will be accomplished. No storm, no tempest of this world or of life will stop the purposes of God. It should be the conviction of every disciple of Christ that when He gives direction, there will be a completion—no matter what. The prophet asks, "Has He spoken and will He not make it good?" (Numbers 23:19). God watches over His word to perform it (Jeremiah 1:12 YLT). It must be our conviction that when given direction from the Lord, that even though it is tested, we must have faith in God's direction.

The great faith chapter, Hebrews 11, is an incredible walk through the halls of faith. We are reminded of the great heroes of faith. Their names trigger our imaginations as we see them in our minds eye doing the incredible acts of faith that qualified them for being mentioned in scripture and thus remembered forever. For over 34 verses this chapter rings with victory and overcoming faith. Then, it takes an interesting turn. It also tells of how "others had trial of mockings and scourgings, yes, and of chains and imprisonment. They were stoned, they were sawn in two, were tempted, were slain with the sword. They wandered about in sheepskins and goatskins, being destitute, afflicted, tormented—of whom the world was not worthy. They wandered in deserts and mountains, in dens and caves of the earth. And all these, having obtained a good testimony through faith, did not receive the promise, God having provided something better for us that they should not be made perfect apart from us."

We see that faith includes testing. The word "testimony" is used in this passage. It's been said that in order to have a testimony you had to go through a test. The testimony is what you have when you successfully pass a test. Up to this point, the message of faith verses from 1-34 is enthusiastic and inspiring, but in verse 35 this is where a shift in gears begins and the message of faith changes. As you study the lives of Joseph, Jacob, Abraham, and Moses, you see that their lives were full of testing! But here is where the message of faith gets in our faces. When the scriptures say, "Others were tortured, not accepting deliverance, that they might obtain a better resurrection," I feel like a 'faith-wimp'.

These great faith champions make up the "great cloud of witnesses" mentioned in Hebrews 12, who may be looking down on us and cheering us on to now follow their example, lay aside every weight, every sin, all the things that can easily ensnare us and run with endurance the race that is set before us.

If all these inspiring stories and people aren't enough, the bible calls us to look unto Jesus, the Author and the Finisher, in other words the prototype of our faith. Even though Jesus Christ was tempted and tested in many ways, His most potent test was by far the Cross. But what does the cross represent? It represents testing.

James 1:2-4 says, " My brethren, count it all joy when you fall into various trials..." All my life, I have hated that scripture. It is one of my least favorite scriptures in the Bible.

You want to know why? Because it is so hard to do! But as much as I dislike the passage, I am convinced that I need it desperately. I need it because of the benefits that come to my life if I respond properly to the dealings of God. Benefits like patience, maturity and completeness are added to my life when I pass the tests of my faith.

My dear friend, Wendell Smith, knows what it means to have his faith tested. He is the founding pastor of The City Church, one of the most influential churches in the nation, and his personal influence and ministry touches hundreds of thousands of Christians and thousands of pastors and churches around the world. He has even written a wonderful book on the subject of faith entitled, *Great Faith*. His own life and the church he founded is marked by great faith. Yet, with all the accomplishments and testimonies of faith, blessing, and success, Pastor Wendell knows firsthand what tremendous tests are like. Several years ago he was diagnosed with a rare blood cancer that is usually detected in elderly people at the end of their lives. Yet, in the prime of his life and ministry, the devil has struck at my friend's health. Though the initial shock of the diagnosis was difficult, Wendell and his wonderful wife Gini, have not flinched in the face of the devil's onslaught. They continue to preach the goodness of God, the blessing of the kingdom, and the glorious Good News of the gospel. They are unabated, undeterred, and unfailing in their faith. In spite of the tremendous test, they are remaining strong in faith.

Maybe you're a little like me and have wondered what in the world God is up to when He tests our faith. Because I'm convinced God is good—I believe that any test that comes my way is there for my good. Did you catch that? Any test that comes your way is there for your good. God wants to make us mature. He wants to make us strong. He wants to help us grow. He wants us to stand in purity and righteousness. That's why the Bible says, "Blessed is the man that endures temptation; for when he has been approved, he will receive the crown of life which the Lord has promised to those who love Him." (James 1:12) In the original language of the text, the word 'temptation' in verse twelve and the word 'trials' in verse two is the same word.

The various trials and temptations that you experience in your life is the testing of your faith. We face all kinds of trials—did not get that promotion, got laid off, the fight you had with your spouse, that bad report you got from the doctor, that relationship you are trying hard to stay pure in. All of these are tests, temptations, or trials.

There are two basic aspects to testing. Both involve the development of our character. The first aspect concerns temptation. Temptation to sin comes from your own carnal desires combined with the things the devil brings into your life to tempt you. The second kind of testing is adversity. Adversity is affliction, resistance, or trouble, they are all allowed by God to test us. Both aspects of testing serve to prove our character, faith and holiness.

That's Not Fair!

Fairness is not always God's method when testing our faith. Many of us go through things in life that do not seem fair. I have a deaf and autistic son. That doesn't seem fair. I have always lived a dedicated life to the Lord. I have never backslidden or gone prodigal on Him. I have given my life to the ministry, preaching the gospel, and building His church. Is this how He rewards His servants? It doesn't seem fair. But fairness is not God's goal—maturity and growth are His goal. Maybe you are enduring a time of testing or adversity and you have those moments when your mind flashes to the it's-not-fair mode. Remind yourself that fairness is not God's goal—growth and maturity are always what He is trying to bring into your life.

Faith For The Process

I had the privilege of going to an educational camp with my son Tyson and we had a great time. One of the activities was making candles. A lady handed us an eight inch string and expected us to go make a candle. My son, who is deaf and autistic, took one look at the string and made a facial expression that said "Hello! What is the deal here?" There were cans of melted wax on a table. Each can had a different color of wax. We dipped the string into the wax, raised it up, allowed it to drip off, then put it in water so it would cool, and then quickly dipped it into the wax again. We did this over and over and over. I remember, standing there after had I dipped the string the first time and noticed the absolute wimpy amount of wax that was on it and I thought, "Wow! We are going to be here until dinner! What is up with that?!" Tyson looked at me as he dipped his string and he started laughing at me. We dipped the string in the wax and in the water for 30 minutes and slowly the candle got bigger and bigger. We noticed that we could mold it because it was still warm and soft. So we began shaping it, spiraling it around and doing different things with it. Once we were finished with the process we had cool candles to take home as a keepsake from camp. There is a moral to this story. God's maturity plan involves a process. Anything you make always involves a process.

Process is not a popular concept to our instant world. In our technology filled world, things are very accelerated. Think about it. We have instant oatmeal, minute rice, and microwave popcorn. Murder mysteries and crime dramas are solved in 42 minutes on television (minus commercials). Our lifestyles do not facilitate process. But that is exactly what God uses when testing our faith. That process with the candle really taught me something about the character of God. The wick represents our lives. The wax represents the character God wants to add to make us useful for His purpose. God will allow us to be dropped into a "hot" situation. In that place of testing God adds to our life the wax (character qualities) and then begins to shape and mold us for His purpose.

Then you have to wait. You can't use it right away. You have to wait until it hardens and then you finally have a candle. Now all of that process is just for a candle. Think about a person's life! You see, the purpose of the candles are many, they give light, aroma, decoration, just like God has a purpose for your life. There is a process of preparation that God needs to take you through in order for that purpose to be fulfilled. That process involves heat and fire, melting, hot and cold, hot and cold.

Have you ever wondered, "God, what in the world are you trying to do to me?!" In Romans 8 we read the scripture, "...for we know that all things work together for good to those who love God, to those who are the called according to His purpose". Have you understood the context of that scripture? Romans 8:18-19 "For I consider that the sufferings of this present time are not worthy to be compared with the glory which shall be revealed in us." The context is suffering and testing that God uses for His purpose—His glory revealed in us.

It is a popular fad these days to have an arm band that states your commitment to a particular cause. The "Be Strong" arm band was popularized by Lance Armstrong, six time Tour de France bike racing champion. His amazing accomplishment of winning the Tour de France happened after he survived testicular cancer. To win once is an amazing feat, but to win six times in a row is just mind boggling and stunning. Do you think it was easy for Lance to do that? For 27 days they ride. It is incredible, all of that work, all of that sweat, all of that endurance. It has been said that the Tour de France is the ultimate physical test. Yet, for all the training and mental strength that it took to propel him to the champions platform, Lance Armstrong attributes much of his cycling success to his physical test of facing cancer. It was the lessons he learned about pain, life, death, strength, endurance—that enabled him to face the limits of his physical strength and push on to victory. Think of all the tests you have gone through in your life... a miscarriage, the loss of a child, the diagnosis of a life-threatening disease. Yet in all those tests we can take hope in the knowledge that God will not allow you to be tested beyond what you are able to handle.

I Corinthians 10:13 "No temptation (no test) has over-taken you except such as is common to man; but God is faithful who will not allow you to be tempted (tested) beyond what you are able, but with the temptation (testing) will also make the way of *escape*, that you may be able to bear it." Many people like to put a period after the word *escape*, but that is not what the bible teaches. When we do that we are saying to God, "Okay God, get me out of here, get me out of this problem!" The scripture actually says that God is going to give you the ability to bear up *through* it. He does not want to remove the test, but give you the strength to pass the test and grow in character. He is after your character devel-opment—the shaping of righteousness and holiness in your life. Be comforted! God _will not_ let you go into a situation that is way over your head and leave you there by yourself. It won't happen! In every test, God will always be there for you. He will make a way of escape for you and that way of escape is the presence and power to be able to do what you need to handle and bear it. Isaiah 30:20-21 "And though the Lord gives you the _bread of adversity and the water of affliction_, yet, your teachers will not be moved into a corner anymore, but your eyes shall see your teachers. Your ears shall hear a word behind you, saying, "This is the way, walk in it." Whenever you turn to the right hand or whenever you turn to the left, that 'voice behind you' is the direction of the Holy Spirit in your life. God is faithful to direct us and help us respond properly to the tests and challenges of life.

Some people struggle with their tests as though something out of the ordinary has happened. 1 Corinthians 10:13 speaks of our time of testing as something that is "common to man…" Elsewhere, the bible tells us, "Beloved, _do not think it strange_ concerning the fiery trials which is to try you, as though some strange (weird or bizarre) thing (has) happened to you;" (1 Peter 4:12) Don't be shocked, don't be taken by surprise, and don't say, "What in the world is going on? I'm entitled to the perfect life!" We must understand what God is doing. He is working on our character.

The Power of His Grace

The "way of escape" for temptation or testing is God's grace. A simple definition of grace is: the God given desire and ability to do His will. Some define grace as God's unmerited favor, but that is a narrow and limited definition because grace is much more than that. It is His enablement—His power. The Greek word for grace (*karis*) is the root of the bible words like power, anointing, and the word 'charisma'. It's how we are able to have the power to do all we do for God. God gives us the grace (power) to do it.

How Character Is Formed

The chart titled, 'How Character is Formed', is a graphic illustration of God's character forming process. On the left side is the God Head of the Trinity and on the right is The World and all of its behavioral ways.

Man stands below and between each of these influences going about a happy-go-lucky life, until he is hit with a problem or situation, an irritation, something you would rather not have...a test!! Now Man is faced with two choices on how to deal with the irritating test. He can choose to React – which is the world's way, or he can choose to Respond – which is God's way. God wants you to be a Responder.

The highlighted 'G' represents God's measure of grace. When we find ourselves with problems and facing a difficult situation in life, Hebrews 4:16 says "Let us come boldly to the throne of grace, that we may obtain mercy and grace to help in time of need." We need to pray and ask God to give us the grace to help handle the situation.

The Word of God is our *response manual* for life. It is God's will and contains God's solutions to every situation, every irritation and every test that will pass through our life.

How Character is Formed

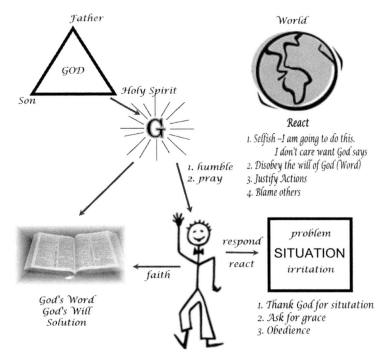

"And be not conformed to this world: but be ye transformed
by the renewing of your mind, that ye may prove... will of God."

Romans 12:2

Reacting VS Responding

When we react to a situation it is almost always charac-
terized by self-centered thoughts and statements like:

"I don't care what the Bible says!"

"I'm going to do this!"

"I don't care what the circumstances are!"

"If she leaves me, fine!"

"I don't care what happens!"

If we are not careful, we can fall into the trap of self-centered thinking rather than handling the situation right and allowing God's character to be formed in our life.

When we follow our selfish desires we will disobey the will of God. When God's Word says, 'forgive' and we don't, or when God's Word says, 'flee sexual immorality' and we don't—we are disobeying the mandates of God's Word. When God's Word says 'humble ourselves', but we don't, instead of receiving grace we discover that God Himself is resisting us (1 Peter 5:5).

Too often we can also justify our actions, which should be a signal that we are reacting to the situation, comment or irritation. While I was in college, I had summer employment at a convenience store. One of the employees had something stolen from them and assumed it was one of his co-workers. While we were in the break room, he stole something out of the jacket of the other person and said, "If he can do it to me, I can do it to him!" How many people do you know who live by this code? As a Christian, you cannot justify your reactions or selfishness—no matter what has been done to you!

Responding to life's irritations and frustration is a whole other ball game. Instead of thinking selfish and self-centered thoughts—we think about how we can serve others and humbly help other people. Instead of becoming frustrated and angry, a Responder will gain control over his anger and express their concerns with self-control. When they are taken advantage of, the Responder will allow the Lord to defend them and will maintain an attitude of trust in God's justice. One of the great expressions of a Responder is when they actually thank God for the irritation as an opportunity to grow in character!!

This is real life stuff. We live this all the time. We can choose to react or respond. To be able to be a Responder we need to humble ourselves, pray, and ask God for grace.

Flavors of Grace

The Bible speaks about diverse kinds of grace (1 Peter 4:10). It is referring to the many kinds of grace that we receive for the different tests of our faith. It's kind of like going to Baskin Robbins with its diversity of ice cream flavors. God has a huge assortment of graces. If you have a bad report from your Doctor, God can give you grace for your health. If you are dealing with anger in a situation, you can ask God to give you grace for that anger and God says, "Here you go! Here is grace for your anger problem." If you are dealing with lust in your heart or lying about something—what ever your need—God has that type of grace for you. So come boldly to the throne of grace, and ask, "Lord, please give me grace for (fill in the blank)".

Keys to Pass the Test of Faith:

1. **You need to *expect to be tested!*** You will even be tested today and have a chance to put into practice what you have just read. Don't be shocked by it or surprised. Don't think some alien thing is happening. Simply expect for tests to come. We're not talking about pessimism or cynicism, but rather an honest and real life understanding that you will experience a test.

2. **Maintain a *positive faith attitude*** because <u>attitude is everything</u>! Faith is your secret weapon during testing. Faith is another word for believe. There are some things you have to believe as you go through a test. Faith and testing come together in times when

you are facing a bad report, fighting a sickness or if you lose your job – you must believe in the goodness of God. Don't go around with your head hanging down saying, 'God, why did you get me fired from my job?' You are reacting to the situation and blaming others. It is not God's fault you lost your job, it may be your fault or the result of a character problem in you that God is dealing with. Or it may simply be the economic challenges of your work sector. Because God is so good, He is going to give you the grace to get that issue worked out, and you will get another job, and you will keep it because you fixed the character problem. You must believe that God is good. You must believe God will work each problem out for good. Envision or imagine the good. See it. Confess this truth: *My character is being developed and I will be a better person because of the test.* You must believe, and remind yourself, there are benefits to testing, such as patience, purity, genuine faith, holiness, perseverance, character, hope, maturity and the crown of life! These are rewards for those who pass the test with faith. Your faith often depends on what you choose to think of. You need to choose to "set your mind on the things that are above".

3. *Ask for grace* to pass the test, to overcome that situation, or to break a habit. You need God's power to pass the test, so ask for it!! God will give you what you need to come through that situation like a winner! Be specific about the kind of grace you need—and ask for it! You will receive it! If you need grace for kicking that drug habit, then ask God for "kick-the-drug-habit" grace! The bible tells us that we can receive "grace *to help*". That's why we need grace—it's there to help us! Ask for it.

4. *Obey God's Word.* His Word is His Response Manual to the tests of life. Once we have asked for grace, we have received it and we must act on it. Years ago Cheerios brand cereal ran a television ad with a big letter "G" and the little Cheerio next to it. The voice-over declared, "Big 'G'—little 'o': Go Power!" And millions of people made Cheerios their choice for breakfast. The big 'G' represents God's grace. The little 'o' is our obedience. Lots of grace and our obe-

dience help us to go forward to maturity in life. This formula will help you be a Responder instead of a Reactor.

5. *Don't give up!* I'm convinced that so many people give up right at the end of the test – within sight of the finish line. They just lay down on the road saying "I've decided I am not going to do this anymore." And you wish you could just go over and wake them up saying, "Come on, it is right there! You can make it! Don't give up!" So if you are weary with the test of your faith—let me encourage you: Don't give up!! You're gonna make it! Keep going! Press on! The end of the test is just ahead!

6. *Trust God!* A person in my church was diagnosed with cancer and the Lord gave me this phrase for her, "We trust in you Lord, we trust in you Lord!" And as I stood over her. I declared these words to her, "We trust in you Lord, we trust in you Lord!" Psalm 37: 3–8, 18 "Trust in the Lord, and do good; dwell in the land, and feed upon His faithfulness. Delight yourself also in the Lord, and He shall give you the desires of

your heart. Commit your way to the Lord, trust also in Him, and He shall bring it to pass. He shall bring forth your righteousness as the light, and your justice as the noonday. Rest in the Lord, and wait patiently for Him; do not fret because of him who prospers in his way, because of the man who brings wicked schemes to pass." Some of you are in a test and may need this next one, "Cease from anger and forsake wrath; do not fret—it only causes harm."

Verse 18 says, "The Lord knows the days of the upright." Have you ever thought, 'The Lord has no clue what is going on here. If He did, this would not be happening to me!'? "The Lord knows the days of the upright, and their inheritance shall be forever." The Lord *does know* what is happening. He will draw near to you and help you.

Verse 23 "The steps of a good man are ordered (established) by the Lord, and He delights in his way." God is trying to work some good things into your life. This test may have aspects that are excruciating, but as you continue through this test, God is ordering your steps. He is causing order to come into the chaos. He is putting things in their place so they will work together for your good!

Verse 24 "Though he fall, he shall not be utterly cast down; for the Lord upholds him with His hand."

Verse 39-40 "But the salvation of the righteous is from the Lord; He is their strength in the time of trouble. And the Lord shall help them and deliver them; He shall deliver them from the wicked, and save them, because they trust in Him."

Remember the Word for the sick woman, "We trust you Lord"? You can say, "I don't understand what's going on. I don't have all the answers, and frankly, I am confused, but one thing I do know: "I trust you!" Have you ever been in those situations in life? Times when you are confused? When you don't have answers and you don't have any direction?

Friend, you can trust the Lord! Your times are in His hand. Nothing is happening to you that He cannot handle. Though you are going through a test of faith, remember the goodness of the Lord and He will sustain you. On your sick bed you will receive strength and encouragement from the Holy Spirit.

Even in your time of discouragement or despair, He will lift you up and set your feet upon a Rock and you shall not be moved!! You have received faith from the Author of faith, now believe that this test, this situation will turn out for your good. Activate your faith by confessing God's good intentions for you. Give Him thanks for the opportunity to grow in character and become more like Christ! Ask for the grace that you need and God will supply it. You watch—you will pass this test!

Chapter 4
Faith to Move Mountains

"For assuredly, I say to you, whoever says to this mountain, 'Be removed and be cast into the sea,' and does not doubt in his heart, but believes that those things he says will be done, he will have whatever he says."

Mark 11:23

I was standing in the living room when I felt it. It was faint...distant. But it was there. A tremor moving through the room, barely perceptible, yet distinct. At the moment I assumed it was a minor earthquake. I soon would find out it was something much more. The day was May 18, 1980. Mt. St. Helens would forever be changed.

Our state's rumbling volcano had literally been "moved" by an explosion of such force that it spewed volcanic ash into the highest strata of our atmosphere. The ash cloud would circle the earth and in some parts of our state, block out the sun in mid-day. It was almost apocalyptic. It was certainly unforgettable. To see a mountain literally move from its foundation – heaved into the air by force – is a miracle of nature. But there are supernatural ways God moves mountains in the lives of people. Every time I see or hear of these amazing stories, it is equally as jaw-dropping.

All of us have mountains in our lives—obstacles to what we believe to be the plan and purpose of God. Some of these mountains God desires us to climb. He doesn't want to remove the challenge, but uses it to make us stronger people. There are other mountains that God wants to move. It is these challenges to our faith that require nothing short of a miracle. The miracle of mountain – moving faith.

Jesus was hungry at one point and looked for some fruit to eat from a fig tree. When he searched the tree for food, but found none, he cursed the tree and it died. His disciples were amazed to see this and Jesus told them that if they had the faith of only the size of a mustard seed they could speak to a mountain to be cast into the sea and it would be done. The one requirement? "Have faith in God."

Between You and Your Desires

In this story Jesus is just confronted simply with a desire. He's hungry. He wanted some food. He wanted figs. He wanted figs off that fig tree and he wanted them right now. He went to the fig tree, took a look, and there were no figs on the tree.

I believe there are some of you reading this book right now that have some desires in your heart, but there is a mountain between you and your desires—some obstacle that is in the way of fulfilling those desires. What are you going to do about this mountain? What about those desires? Too often people surrender to the mountain instead of making the mountain surrender to them. What about you?

To Be or Not To Be

Someone reading this is probably wondering, "But what if it is not God's will for me to have that desire fulfilled?" I get it. It's a very normal thing to think. Are my desires 'to be or not to be'? It's not as though I'm asking to solve world hunger or bring world peace. It's just a desire. No global crisis or threat to humanity—just my desires.

Now there are desires that God wants you to overcome. Sinful desires (known as lust in the bible) are to be dealt with and overcome. We are not to tolerate sinful desires. But are there desires that are proper to have and even to pray that they be fulfilled? The answer is an unequivocal—yes!!

A Loving, Good Heavenly Father

I can't tell you how many times I've gone to the store with one of my kids, only to have their desires ringing in my ears within 5 seconds of entering the store! And, you know it, they ask and they receive. Why? Because I love them. As much as lies within me I want to give them what they desire. There are times I say "No" in order to teach them to wait or save their own money. Sometimes I will say "No" because I am planning on giving it to them at Christmas or for their birthday. Every parent knows what I'm talking about because you love your kids. The scripture says, "If you, then, being evil, know how to give good gifts to your children, how much more will your Father who is in heaven give good things to those who ask Him?" (Matthew 7:11 NKJV) Your loving heavenly Father thoroughly loves to bless His kids. As one of His children, you can expect for God to respond to your prayer of faith to move the mountain that separates you from your desires.

Your Mountain and Your Need

One day a demon possessed child was brought to the disciples, but they could not cast out the demon. They brought the child to Jesus who took authority over the demon and cast it out bringing deliverance to the child. The disciples asked Jesus why they were unable to cast out the demon and again the Lord spoke about faith and its power to move a mountain. The "mountain" in this case was the deliverance of the child. For you, it may be a miraculous breakthrough in your marriage. Your mountain may be that prodigal son or daughter who is away from God, wasting their life in sin. The mountain in these situations is not just a matter of desire, but of desperate need.

What Is Your Mountain?

I believe God wants you to operate in another realm of faith that you may not have walked in before. There are mountains that all of us face. Whether they are obstacles to desires or desperate needs – every person has a mountain that must be moved in order to see those things become reality.

Let me ask you, "What is your mountain? What is it that you are facing? What is it that is in your life that you are contending with—that is keeping you back from receiving your blessing or breakthrough?"

Consider this definition of a mountain and maybe it can help you understand a little bit more about what we are talking about. *A mountain is an impossible situation or an immovable obstacle to your progress or future that requires a miracle to remove it and to continue on toward your destiny.* I'm speaking of something that requires a miracle for it to be removed. It's impossible. It's a big obstacle and an impossible situation. A mountain is between where you are and where you want to go. It is a hindrance to what you feel is supposed to be there for you and your future. It is the circumstance separating you from what you're supposed to be experiencing now in your life.

There are all kinds of mountains in life. For example, a mountain could be a difficult or a painful situation. Maybe a business deal went bad and you're left holding the bag of five thousand, ten thousand, twenty thousand or more dollars. For some, your circumstances are completely beyond your control and now you are stuck with something that has happened to you. You might have an addiction or a habit— something that is plaguing your life and you are chained to that thing. It's like a prison, it's like chains, it's like being in bondage in some way in your life. Friend, God has the power to move that mountain out of your life. For others, it is a condition of your spirit that you are dealing with. Maybe it's depression or prolonged discouragement. You might have a broken or a fractured relationship where some kind of destruction or brokenness has come to your relationship. You have lost hope for repair in the relationship unless a miracle takes place. That is a huge mountain. I know of people who are facing tremendous financial challenges or lack. Still others are dealing with some sickness, disease, or physical challenge. Or maybe you identified with the story of that child's demonic attack and you are battling against some kind of oppression or demonic activity in your life and the enemy is attacking you and coming against you. The list of personal mountains is endless. But the power of our heavenly Father is equal to the challenge of your mountain!! Greater is He that is in you than the mountain you are facing down!!!

How NOT to Do It

There is an instance in the Bible where God uses someone to speak to a mountain. Moses is told by God to speak to a rock mountain and water comes out when he obeys the

Lord (Numbers 20:1-13). Yet even though this miracle takes place, how Moses handles his mountain is a lesson to all of us of how NOT to deal with the mountains in our lives.

1. **Do Not Complain!** The location of this story is a place called Kadesh Meribah, which means "waters of striving." How many of us when faced with mountains in our lives have had a complaining attitude and a complaining spirit? Too often we begin to strive and contend with the Lord, and we whine about how bad it is and how horrible it is, rather than rising up in a spirit of faith and speaking to the mountain. Complaining is spoken unbelief. It is confessed doubt and faithlessness. This is the single greatest reason for God's people failing to possess their Promised Land! How many people are we around who complain a lot? The crazy truth about complaining is that you get what you complain about! I have heard people complain about not having enough finances in their life and guess what? They continue to not have enough finances in their life. Too many people are under the illusion that their complaining changes things. Not true. Complaining often reinforces the reality of

our lives! If we want it to change we must change it with the powerful spirit of faith and a faith-filled confession. Our words must change from complaint to commend. From negative to positive. From doubt to faith.

2. **Do Not React!** What was Moses' mountain? In the biblical account several things happen. First, Moses' sister, Miriam, dies. What a horrible thing to have to experience. Part of Moses' struggle is the pain and grief of the loss of his older sister.

To add insult to injury, the people he is leading begin to accuse him of bringing them out into the wilderness to die!! The same man who is responsible for bringing them out of Egypt by God's mighty hand, parting the Red Sea, and performing wonders and miracles for their good!! All of these things come together and overwhelm Moses. Have you ever felt like everything happening is set against you? I'm sure Moses felt this way.

Now here's how Moses handles the mountain. He reacts to his circumstances out of anger. When faced with testing we are to *respond*, NOT *react*. God told

Moses to "speak to the rock." Instead, Moses reacted to the people and spoke to them out of his pain and declares, "Hear now you rebels!" In Psalm 106:33 this is what the Bible says about Moses' actions here. "Because they rebelled... [Moses] spoke rashly with his lips." The word rashly means thoughtlessly or reacting. He blew up at the situation in his heart, his attitude, and in his anger. Some Bible commentators believe this is the same thing that Jesus is talking about in Matthew 5 when he says, "Whoever says to his brother *Raccah*, or you fool is in danger of hell-fire." Jesus is speaking about reacting out of anger, speaking things that are wrong and tolerating wrong attitudes in our heart.

Moses' attitude became bitter and disrespectful to God's people. Then, Moses strikes the rock—not once, but twice—directly disobeying God's directions to him. There are irritating and frustrating qualities to the mountains that confront us. Don't react, but respond in faith and grace.

3. Don't Take Matters Into Your Own Hands! Moses striking the rock is a symbol of him taking matters into his own hands. He even says, "Must we bring water for you out of this rock?" As if he has the power in himself to make this happen. Moses is basically saying, "I'm going to show you! I'm going to deal with this thing. It's not being dealt with so I'm going to make it happen!"

This is where things get interesting. Does water come out of the rock when Moses strikes it? Yes it does. In this lies the danger of taking matters into your own hands—sometimes your self-effort will appear to work. So we keep trying things in our own strength, and this is where the deception comes in. We subtly deceive ourselves into thinking we can handle this mountain on our own strength. On the occasions when it goes right, we even take the credit—"You see, I can do this!" Not realizing that we are taking the glory for our success, instead of giving glory to God. This is one of the subtle traps of pride and self reliance.

God says something to Moses that reveals the core issue. Numbers 20:12 says, "Because you didn't believe in Me…", a phrase that rebukes Moses for his lack of faith. Moses taking matters into his own hands was a declaration that he did not trust God nor believe that He would deal with this difficult situation. Think about that the next time you are tempted to take matters into your own hands.

Consequences

Moses is then rebuked by God for taking matters into his own hands and for failing to believe Him as he faced his mountain. As a result, the powerful consequence is that he will not be able to bring God's people into the Promised Land. It was one of the great goals of his life and, now, he was not going to be able to fulfill it. All because he failed to face his mountain in faith.

My friend, it is absolutely crucial that you handle the mountains in your life in the right spirit and with the right attitude. Mishandling your attitude and emotions can lead to reactions that will bring about tragic results. The fruit of our complaining and negativity can even affect our destiny.

Keys To Overcoming Your Mountain

Every mountain climber must have the right equipment if he is to climb the mountain. Several years ago my father-in-law and I, along with a guide climbed to the peak of Mt.

Hood in Oregon. It was amazing to stand atop the summit and see the spectacular view. The feeling of accomplishment also came with a sense of victory—we had conquered the mountain. But before we had even set foot on that mountain, there had been hours of preparation and the gathering of all the tools and equipment we would need to scale the mountain. As you face the struggles and challenges of mountains in your life, you will need tools and equipment, principles for conquering the mountain you are facing.

1. Make God BIG!

David knew a thing or two about overcoming challenges. Once when facing an impossible situation he calls fellow mountain-movers to "Magnify the Lord with me" (Psalm 34:3 NKJV). What do you do when you magnify something? You make it big. Through a certain type of focus you make it big and you change your perspective on the object. That's what you do when you magnify the Lord. When you worship Him you are hallowing Him. You are making Him big; you are making Him special in your eyes.

God's not up in heaven on some ego trip and needs to be made to feel special. But He knows that if you make

Him special in your eyes, *your perspective changes.*
Something happens to you—in you. Notice the perspective David gains as he makes God big! "I sought the Lord,
and He heard me, and delivered me from all my fears.
They looked to Him and were radiant, and their faces
were not ashamed. This poor man cried out, and the Lord
heard him, and saved him out of all his troubles." (Psalm
34:4-6 NKJV) Later he declares, "Oh, taste and see that
the Lord is good; Blessed is the man who trusts in Him!"
(Psalm 34:8 NKJV)

Too many people say, "Oh, but you don't understand!
My mountain is BIG. It's a nasty, brutal mountain. Its
face is insurmountable. Its strength is indomitable. I have
never seen anything so great as this! I've been dealing
with this thing for ages." And I would say to you, "Stop
magnifying your mountain!" You are telling me all about
your mountain. You're telling me about all of its intrica-
cies. You're telling me about all of its caves and all of
its shadows. You're telling me about all of the storms
you have experienced as you've been at the base of that
mountain. You're telling me about how big it is, how tall
it is. What's your focus? The mountain?! What does the
Bible say? "Magnify THE LORD!" Stop focusing on the

mountain. Focus on the Lord that moves the mountain. Focus on the Mountain Mover!! Acknowledge Him and His power. Declare His goodness. Confess His Lordship, "I believe you are Lord over this mountain!" What do we do in worship? We declare the Lordship of Jesus. Be a person who says, "God, I know you are Lord. I may not feel like you are Lord. I may not feel like this mountain understands you are Lord, but I know you are the Lord! Whether the mountain knows it or not, You are Lord!" Worship Him. When you hallow the Lord, when you worship Him, when you give Him glory—then amazing things happen. There are stories in the Bible about how God's people are totally, completely, miraculously, and utterly delivered because they simply magnified the Lord. As you magnify the Lord, He takes His rightful place and the mountain takes its proper place—Big God; little mountain!

2. Face the Mountain in Faith!

In Mark 11:22, Jesus is teaching his disciples about facing their mountains and He says, "Have faith in God." This was not a quaint suggestion, but rather a command. In the original text it is an imperative. It is an absolute command requiring full obedience on the part of all hearers. Basically what He is saying is, "Don't have faith in yourself." Don't have faith in your own resources. Don't have faith in your own experience or education. Don't have faith in your own ability. Don't have faith in anything else other than God. Other things might help. Other things might be tools to help you, but that's all they are—just some little things to help you. But when it comes to moving mountains, God is the One Who's going to move it. Have faith in God. It's God's power. It's God's will that's at work in your situation.

Also when He says, "have faith in God," He's saying don't let frustration rule your spirit. Let faith rule. You may have been struggling with this mountain for a long time. You may have antagonists and detractors. But don't become frustrated! Frustration is a condition of weakened faith. Let me say that again. Frustration is a condition of weakened faith. Strengthen your faith! Renew and rejuvenate your faith!

How do we do this? The scriptures tell us that faith comes by hearing the word of God (Romans 10:17). Look at your mountain and ask, "What does the Word say?" Saturate your mind with the Word of God. Pray until you receive a 'rhema' (Spirit-given) word from God. Pray and ask God to quicken a Scripture to you. Ask Him to make it come alive to you and go, "Man that is it! I need to believe for that!" What does the Word say? Wait in prayer. Listen to the voice of the Spirit. Do what Moses did and place yourself before the Lord until God speaks, and then when you have direction, confront your mountain. You're going to build faith to deal with that mountain by getting a word. Some of you just need to believe the Bible. You don't need some burning bush experience. You just need to believe what it says. Read scriptures that build your faith to deal with your mountain, and then speak to the mountain and it will move. Too many believers have dirt-clod faith. They have about as much faith as it takes to move a dirt clod. But friend, you are facing a mountain here!! Your dirt clod faith isn't going to move that mountain. You need mountain moving faith that is inspired by the mountain moving promises of the Word of God!! And once you have the word—act on it!

3. Speak to Your Mountain!

Jesus said in Mark 11, "For assuredly I say unto you whoever *says* to this mountain be removed and be cast into the sea..."(Italics added). Speak what you've heard. Declare the Word of the Lord. Prophesy to your mountain. Some people say, "I don't know what to say!" What did God tell you? Let me ask you this, what do you want Him to do? How many times did people come to Jesus for something and what was Jesus' response? "What do you want me to do for you?" Well, let me ask you, "What would you want Him to do for you?" Maybe your response is, "Well, I would really like God to give me another job that has better benefits and better pay, and to really help me into a better financial situation." There you go! Speak your desires!

Get alone with God, set that mountain in front of you and say, "In the name of Jesus I declare that I'm going to have a better job. I believe that Your word says You want to bless me. You want to prosper me. Joshua 1:8-9 says that if I have this Word in my heart and not turn from it to the right or to the left that You will prosper me wherever I go and give me good success. I believe Your Word! Right now I declare that either I will get promoted in my job or get a better job! I believe You Lord—that You are going to move this mountain!"

What do you want me to do for you? That is what God is saying. What do you want? What have you heard from God? Maybe you're dealing with sickness or some infirmity. Begin declaring these things to your mountain. "I am healed in the name of Jesus! I know that Jesus went about doing good and healing all who were oppressed of the devil (Acts 10:38). The same Spirit that raised Christ Jesus from the dead dwells in me and He will quicken my mortal body and my mortal body will be changed in a moment (Romans 8:11). That same Holy Spirit is in me and now is working in me and I command my body, by the power of the Holy Spirit, to be healed!"

Some people have said, "You're bossing God around. You're just treating Him like your errand boy." No, I'm not. I'm speaking to the mountain! I am not commanding God. The mountain is the subject of my command and God is the Source of the command! I am prophesying to the mountain! I'm declaring to that sickness "Come out of that person and be healed in Jesus' Name. I see you and you are a healed, living, vibrant, energetic person by the name of Jesus!!" Don't reason about the mountain—prophesy to it!! Declare the word of the Lord over your mountain and watch it move!!

4. Do Not Doubt in Your Heart!

What is your heart? Your heart is the place where things are born. I'm talking about your mind. It's where you're vision is. I'm not talking about natural vision; I'm talking about the vision of your soul. It's where you see things. It's where you get something, where you see something before it is ever there naturally. You see it in your heart.

In Joshua 6, God takes Joshua to the walls of Jericho. Joshua knows he is going to take this city and he knows the challenge ahead. It was not an easy task. The walls to the city were high. The army defending the city was strong. The fortifications were great. Notice how God speaks to Joshua. He says, "*See*! I have given Jericho into your hand." What was God doing? He was speaking to Joshua's heart. He was saying, "Joshua *see it*! *See* those walls coming down! *See* those people falling under the hand of God. *See* My hand moving and giving you victory. *See* your army rushing into the city and having victory. *See* these walls falling down flat. *See* the victory of

God! *See* the people dancing and celebrating the victory of God's people. *See* it! *See* yourself wearing the robe of the victor. *See* yourself bringing the spoils of the city and giving them to God. *See* yourself bring all the gold and all of the silver, and all of the bronze, and all of the clothing, and all of the garments, and all of those things in a big mountain, this big heap and turning the mountain that is Jericho into the mountain of inheritance for God!" Bring what you see by faith in your heart out through the declaration of your mouth!

Remember that the walls of Jericho fell down flat because they were spoken to. The walls of Jericho fell down flat because they shouted. They didn't raise a spear. They didn't draw a sword. They spoke to their mountain. But first, Joshua had to see it in his heart.

Don't doubt in your heart. Don't go by what your natural eyes see. Go by what the vision of your heart is. Visualize what you want. Visualize the Word of the Lord coming to pass. Picture it in your mind. Through the days to follow you will be tempted to doubt. Don't give in. Believe what you see with eyes of faith and refuse to entertain those thoughts of doubt.

In my community I have prayed for financial blessing. I have literally prayed over empty fields and property lots and declared businesses that I've seen in my spirit. I have visualized things happening there. I have pictured with the imagination of faith – the prosperity of my community. And I am seeing my prayers come to pass. I am seeing it happen. Today there is a Wal-Mart and Albertsons in a lot I prayed over some years before. Another empty field I prayed over now has a Home Depot and Applebees restaurant in it. I believe it is a direct result of faith-filled prayers. Months and years went by without anything happening, but I continued praying with faith in my heart and did not allow the doubt from contradiction to sway me.

Doubt is most often the child of delay and contradiction. A promise is given or a vision is received and then time marches on bringing delay. Every person has experienced this. Great heroes of faith experienced it. Abraham and Sarah, Jacob and Rachel, Joseph, Moses, Hannah – all experienced the frustration of delay. Combined with contradiction, delay often produces doubt. Contradictions are when the opposite of what is promised happens. A wife receives a promise for a healed marriage only to be confronted with separation papers from her husband. Or a father receives a promise of restoration with his rebellious son only to discover when he comes home from work that his son has become even more prodigal and has left home. Contradictions are very difficult to deal with, and when combined with delay, doubt almost always follows.

Even though delay, contradiction and doubt are all too real for many of us, we cannot allow them to overrule our spirit of faith. Keep your focus on the prize—the vision of God's promise. Time can't cancel God's promise. Contradiction can't cancel God's promise. His word is unchangeable and unalterable. It is never failing. It is contradicted, but not conquered! It is attacked, but not overcome! It is delayed, but not cancelled! It is sure! It is powerful! It is creative! And it shall be accomplished!! Do not doubt!!

5. Believe The Things That You Say Will Be Done!

Notice the words of Jesus in Mark 11, "This is what I say to you, whoever says to this mountain be removed and cast into the sea and does not doubt in his heart *but believes that those things he says will be done* he will have whatever he says." (italics added)

Think about that. "He will have whatever he says," if he "believes that those things he says will be done." The word "done" means "to come or to come into existence; to begin to be or to receive being." It means accomplished events. This word means to arise or to occur in history; to come upon the stage. It speaks concerning miracles— miracles that are in a process of being worked out. It's not necessarily an instantaneous thing. In fact, I want to suggest to you today that "done" is a process word.

Here's how it works. When it says you "believe that those things...will be done", it's as though, in your spirit it is already done, but you're waiting for it to manifest itself in the natural realm. You believe in your spirit that it's already finished. You see it with your spiritual eyes. It's done! But you're waiting for it to manifest itself and so there is time involved. My counsel to you is to be patient. You're facing a mountain and you want it to be gone now. "God just microwave this thing out of my life!" But process is involved and because there's a process there must also be patience. Patient faith is the faith that endures the contradiction without doubting.

You wait in faith for the manifestation of what you see in the spirit!

I believe also that this particular phrase in the Bible is a declaration; it's telling us the power of confession. Think about this: "Believes that those things he says will be done." Just take one part of that verse. "Those things he says will be done." What kind of confession have you been having about your mountain?

"We're never going to get out of here."

"This is killing me."

"I am broke, I've always been broke. I'm always going to be broke. What is the story?"

What is your confession? Let me say this: you have what you say. This is a really big deal. You get what you say and you say what you believe. Think about it. Work backwards from there. If you believe something it will come out of your mouth. "As a man thinks in his heart..." (Proverbs 23:7) and "out of the abundance of the heart the mouth speaks" (Luke 6:45). And here in this scripture it says, "Those things that he says will be done." So think about that. "I'm broke, always been broke, always will be broke." So what's going to happen? You're going to be broke. "Are you talking, Marc, about blabbing it and grabbing it and naming it and claiming it?" No, I am talking about a good confession. I am completely aware of the extremes in the kingdom. It is very clear. The scripture says you have what you say and if you've been saying all this junk about your life and about the mountain your facing that is what you're going to get. So my challenge to you today is to change what you are saying. To do this you must change what you are thinking. Have faith in God. Magnify the Lord and speak to your mountain: "I see you! You are coming down!"

I see a change coming into your spirit—a Holy Spirit boldness and fire that burns in you. A mountain will rise up before you and you're going to be able to stand up and say, "That is not happening! That is not my future! That is not what God has for me! That is not my inheritance. This is my inheritance! This is what God has said: I am healed! I am blessed! The hand of the Lord is on me! I'm going to break through!! I'm going to have victory!!!" You don't need to be a prophet to do that. You just need to be a faith-filled man or woman of God who speaks God's word over your life. Speak to that mountain, "You're out of here!"

Things Are About To Change!

As you put these principles into practice, you will see things change. The landscape will begin to shift before you. It may take some patience and endurance, but they will change.

Mark 11:24 says, "Therefore I say to you whatever things you ask when you pray believe that you receive them and you will have them." It just can't get any clearer than that. And you have a choice today. You can stay at the foot of that mountain and continue to be bound to that mountain. Or you can choose to rise up today, listen to the word of the Lord today, believe it and begin to prophesy to your mountain! Speak to your mountain, picture in your heart what it's like for that thing not to be there. Can you see it? That addiction is gone. That broken relationship is restored. That impossible situation is made right. I'm telling you that a new day will dawn for your future and destiny if you will believe for that mountain to be removed! Receive mountain-moving faith today! Build yourself up in faith and watch as the force of faith blows that mountain away!!

Chapter 5
Faith for When God Says, "No."

"Then God said: "No, Sarah your wife shall bear you a son, and you shall call his name Isaac; I will establish My covenant with him for an everlasting covenant, and with his descendants after him."
Genesis 17:19

He was stunned. My son just looked at me with this look of disbelief. He had asked me for something – it was good and enjoyable. There wasn't really any harm in having it (according to him). And yet, I had said, "No." He began to make his case, presenting his argument like a district attorney. Perspectives were offered. Reasoning was exceptional and yet, I was resolute. "No" was the answer. His shoulders slumped and his head wagged in disagreement as he shuffled off. It was as though he was saying, "This stinks!" Here's the connection for you. Just as your natural father would say, "No" to you, so your heavenly Father will say "No" as well. The big question is, how do you handle it when God says, "No?"

Not Often

I did a word search for the word "No" in the scriptures and I discovered something very interesting. While the word "no" occurs more than 2,000 times in the bible, there are very few times in the Bible where God actually says, "No." It is used by people, men and women, and in stories. It is used to show that there was no longer any grain in the barn, or there was no more people in that city, or no problem that God couldn't solve, or whatever; but there were very few times that God said, "No" to people. That should tell you something about his nature. God is a Giver, a Rewarder (Hebrews 11:6). So as we deal with the times when God does say, "No," we must remember that it is rare.

There was a very difficult challenge that we faced as a church. Without going into the details of the whole story, it was a battle that required a lot of faith and prayer. We gave hours to prayer. Some people fasted and interceded for the breakthrough in the situation, but in the end the situation did not have the result we were asking for. In fact it was the opposite. God had said, "No."

What do you do when that happens? How do you deal with the conflict and confusion that seems to ebb and flow in your heart? How should we process our emotions and feelings about it all? We need answers for when God says, "No" to us, because He *will* say, "No" to us. It will happen. It is in the Bible and it will happen in your life. You will come to God with something and He will say, "No." In spite of all our questions, emotions, and inner conflicts – and all of those things are very real – they need to be handled with a spirit of faith. I'm telling you today that you need to handle God's answer with a spirit of faith.

God's First "No"

When God created Adam and Eve He placed them in the Garden of Eden to care for it. In the Garden were two trees, the Tree of Life and the Tree of the Knowledge of Good and Evil. They had everything they could possibly want and God said "Yes" to it all, except the Tree of the Knowledge of Good and Evil. To that Tree He said, "No." He offered no explanation. He gave no reason. When it came to eating of the Tree of the Knowledge of Good and Evil, God said, "No."

"No" Because of Love

While there is no reason or explanation offered, there is something God makes exceptionally clear: If they eat of the Tree of the Knowledge of Good and Evil they will die. God knows that to eat of it will produce death in Adam and Eve. It was a "No" for their protection. It was also a "No" based on the fact that God knows the future. One of the reasons that God says, "No" to you is because He knows something you don't know about the future. God knows everything. He is omniscient, all knowing. He knows your past. He knows you present. You can say, "I know that. I know my past and I know my present." But here's one thing that He does know that you don't – the future. You don't know the future and He does. He does know what the future holds, and when God says, "No" to you and me, many times He knows that there is something in the future that will harm your life and He says, "No."

My son, Zachary, has always been a picky eater. As a boy, he would snack on different things and then when it was time to eat with the family, he would say, "I'm not hungry."

He would snack on chocolate chip cookies and then not be hungry for dinner. Now, usually if he were to come to us and ask for cookies we would say, "No." Why? Because a steady diet of chocolate chip cookies is not healthy. We would tell him "No" for his own good. There are many other things that are unhealthy or dangerous that our kids can do, so we tell them "No" when they ask. Do you always explain all those things to your kids? No.

God knows when it's not going to be good for you. He knows that you won't die, but that it won't be good. Now from your perspective, it's good, it might even taste good, feel good, or whatever, but it is unhealthy. God knows when things are unhealthy for you, not that it would be "sin," or wrong for you to have it. But he would say, "No" to you because he knows it's unhealthy for your soul, or unhealthy for your spirit.

When it comes to certain personal standards in my life, there are some things that I just don't do, or see, or allow myself to watch because God has said, "No" to me. And the reason why is because He knows that if I go ahead and do that, it's going to be unhealthy for my soul and unhealthy for my spirit. Is it sin? No. There's no verse in the Bible.... "Thou shall not..." There's nothing like that, but to me it would be sin. And if I said, "I don't care what You say, I'm going to do it anyway." Then I would be disobedient, and because God loves me He says, "No." Because He loves me and wants to protect me, He says, "No." Because He wants me to be strong, He says, "No" to me. Because He wants me to be healthy, He says, "No" to me. Because He loves me, He says, "No." I want you to remember that. Because He loves you, He says, "No."

God Is Not Holding Out On You

I think it's really interesting that in spite of God saying, "No," Adam and Eve do it anyway. Have you ever done that? I have. I've had God tell me "No" and I've went ahead and did it anyway. You know what? Every time, I can't think of one single time it was good. It's just horrible. You feel bad and in your heart you know it was bad. It just ends up being bad all the way around. And you think to yourself, "I should not have done that." One of the things that you may assume when God says "No" is that God is holding out on you. When God says, "No" to you, please don't think that. When God says, "No," I'm telling you right now, He's not holding out on you. When you go down that road, what you're really saying is that God is mean and selfish. He is stingy or being miserly with His blessings. He's not being mean. Really what you're saying is that He's a mean God. He's not a good God, but He's a mean God...He's holding out on you. He is not holding out on you. God is good!! What does the bible say? "For the Lord is good and His mercy endures forever!" In other words, He's good how many times? All the time. He is good all the time. Even when He says, "No," He's good. And remember this: He is doing it for your good. Hebrews 11:6 says He's not a God that holds out. He is a Rewarder of those that diligently seek him. When God says, "No" we must handle it with faith and we must believe that God is not holding out on us. We need to assume that, when God says, "No."

No Plan B

In Genesis 17 we see Abraham waiting for what has been promised: a child. But what has been promised isn't happening. He's waiting. He's waiting. He's waiting. Finally, after a lot of waiting and much delay Sarah, his wife, comes up with a plan. She speaks with her husband and says, "Why don't we do this surrogate mother thing. Why don't you lie with my female servant, Hagar. She'll become pregnant. You'll have a son, and God's promise will be fulfilled."

Abraham, tired of waiting for the promise to be fulfilled, gives in to Plan B. Sure enough, Hagar gets pregnant. She gives birth to a son. Abraham calls his name Ishmael. Ishmael is the father of all the Arab nations that we have today, and they still consider Abraham to be their father. Notice God's response to Abraham and Sarah's "plan." In Genesis 17, God comes to Abraham again and says in verse 1, "I am Almighty God, walk before me and be blameless. I will make my covenant between Me and you and will multiply you exceedingly." Abraham's probably thinking "Alright, Ishmael, yes, alright!" Abraham falls to the ground and God talks to him about his future and the promise. God not only renews His promise to Abraham, but to Sarai his wife. "Regarding Sarai, your wife—her name will no longer be Sarai. From now on her name will be Sarah. And I will bless her and give you a son from her! Yes, I will bless her richly, and she will become the mother of many nations. Kings of nations will be among her descendants." (Genesis 17:15-16) Then he fell to the ground and laughed. I think one of the reasons he probably fell and laughed was because he probably thought, "Are you kidding me?!" Then he says, "Shall a child be born to a man that's a hundred years old and shall Sarah, whose ninety years old bare a child?" Then Abraham lifts up this whole

Plan B thing to God, "Oh, that Ishmael might live before you." Then God said, "No, Sarah, your wife shall bare you a son. And you shall call his name Isaac. I will establish my covenant with him for an everlasting covenant."

Right about now, Abraham is feeling pretty small because he has tried plan B; and God said, "No, that's not what I want." Want to know one of the reasons that God says, "No" to us? Because sometimes we're trying to make supernatural things happen with natural strength. We presume that we can do this with fasting. We can think sometimes if we fast enough it'll impress God enough and He'll say, "Wow they're really serious, I better do something about this." No, you fast because God tells you to fast. Not to manipulate God. You read Isaiah 58, where it says, "Is this the fast that I've chosen?" God's people were fasting, but it wasn't for the right reasons, and it wasn't because God told them to. Jesus even condemned the Pharisees for fasting and doing things out of a religious spirit when God had not told them to do it, and they were trying to appear religious and impress people with their religious activities. This is so important. We are faced in our lives with all kinds of challenges—all kinds of things that we need God's help with. The day that you think that you can get out there and figure it out and do it on your own strength is the day God's going to say, "No, I don't want you to do that." He's going to tell you, "No." You know what will happen if you get into the habit of doing it on your own strength? You will continue to live your life where you are the source of your life and He is not. Too many people get frustrated with the delays to the promise. They begin to engineer plans and solutions in the flesh and in the natural. Too often people conjure up natural solutions to circumstances and challenges that need supernatural intervention. When we do this, we place ourselves in the place of God as the Source of our life. Friend, as educated and smart as you are, on your best day, you are not even as wise as the foolishness of God. God's wisdom and strength; His creativity and power is the only resource we must rely on. Our little "Plan B" will not cut it. Don't rashly react to your situation. I plead with you to not try to engineer your own solution. Wait on the Lord. Let Him bring His plans to bear on your situation and you will find success.

"No" For Right Priorities

One of the other reasons God says "No" is when He deals with our priorities. One of the Ten Commandments is, "You will have no other gods before Me." He says, "No" to us to keep our priorities in check. He says, "No" so that our priorities will stay in proper alignment. He'll say, "No" to you because if He says, "Yes" to you, that thing will become more important to you than God. So sometimes God says, "No," in order for you to have your priorities right. That means He wants everything balanced out in your life. He is the reason why we live, and all our purposes for life revolve around Him, and revolve around His plan and His purpose for us. Balanced priorities keep us committed to doing what He wants, and we're able to pray the prayer, "Not my will, but your will be done."

Forcing The Door Will Cost You

I know people that have lost thousands of dollars in business deals because God said, "No." and they did it anyway. I heard a story of a Christian businessman, a multi-millionaire, who decided not to wait on God and forced the issue on a business opportunity. The consequence to his impatience was the loss of almost ten million dollars in the deal. Some of you might be thinking, "It must be nice to have ten million dollars to lose." I guarantee you this business person did not think it was "nice." Because of his impatience, foolishness and coming up with his own "Plan B", he lost ten million dollars. Instead of waiting for God to say, "Yes," he forced the issue and lost. He went back and asked God's forgiveness and acknowledged he was wrong. Of course, God saw his repentant heart and this businessman has worked to honor God and to follow His direction. Because of this change, God has blessed him; and of course he's made back much more than he lost and has been blessed because of the goodness of God. But think of how much more he would have been blessed, if he would have received God's "No" and waited. It will cost you if you force the door on "No." It'll cost you every time. Violating God's "No" can be very expensive.

Some of the strife that's in the Middle East exists because Abraham forced the door on "No." Let's review the story. Genesis 16 tells of Abraham's wife, Sarah, devising a "Plan B" to help God out on a promise He had made to them. She decided that since time was passing them by and she was not getting any younger, that her husband could lay with her Egyptian maid, Hagar. In doing this, Hagar would become pregnant with child and give Abraham and Sarah their promise. They don't check with God first, but rashly follow this foolish plan. Hagar becomes pregnant with a son and gives birth to a boy and calls him Ishmael. He is the ancestor of the Arab nations in the Middle East. Later, in Genesis 17, God appears to Abraham and Sarah and tells them that they will have a son. Abraham tries to negotiate with God by informing the Lord of their 'Plan B'. Genesis 17:15-16 is where God repeats His promise to Abraham.

"Then God said to Abraham, "Regarding Sarai, your wife—her name will no longer be Sarai. From now on her name will be Sarah. And I will bless her and give you a son from her! Yes, I will bless her richly, and she will become the mother of many nations. Kings of nations will be among her descendants." Genesis 17:16-17 NKJV

Now notice Abraham's response:

"Then Abraham bowed down to the ground, but he laughed to himself in disbelief. "How could I become a father at the age of 100?" he thought. "And how can Sarah have a baby when she is ninety years old?" So Abraham said to the Lord, "May Ishmael live under your special blessing!" But God replied, "No—Sarah, your wife, will give birth to a son for you. You will name him Isaac, and I will confirm my covenant with him and his descendants as an everlasting covenant."" Genesis 17:17-19 NKJV

Abraham hears the promise repeated by the Lord and then proceeds to present Plan B to God as a viable option! He has not talked to God about it. It's an option which clearly violates God's directive and promise. Yet, in spite of these things, Abraham throws up Plan B for approval. And what is God's first word on the subject? Let's read the scripture again. Genesis 17:19, "But God replied, "No..."" I love the power of the scriptures. Look at how this is worded. "But God replied..." It's as if the Word of God is making the point I am God and you are not. It's a statement about His authority, His power, and His unchanging promise. Abraham and Sarah, in their tiny human world, with their puny human perspective, made a plan. They decided, in their "wisdom", to outvote the God of the universe—the Creator of heaven and earth. The Author of life and the Promise of all that is to come was outvoted by two people who had been sucking air a mere 100 years. They had a plan. An alternative to the perfect, powerful, God-ordained plan. They hatched Plan B. And God said, "No." (I'm God and you're not!)

I have seen this happen time and again with Christians who get impatient with God's promise and start to engineer an alternative plan. They have waited—many of them for months and years. They watch as seasons come and seasons go, with little or no change to their situation. Nothing seems to be happening and to make matters worse, others with less faith and greater challenges seem to be getting answers and results, while they are stuck on hold. Out of frustration they come up with Plan B – Ishmael. Little do they realize that Ishmael has fruit (children) that will cause trouble later. If they would have just simply followed God's direction and not gotten impatient, they would have the promise fulfilled—without complications. Remember that forcing the door will cost you. It may cost you time, money, energy, or relationships. Or worse still, it may cost you all of these things. Instead, listen to the voice of God. Get His green light for every plan and decision. Obtain His permission. Remember, that God, in His all-wise perspective knows something you don't. He knows the end from the beginning. He knows, and you don't. That means that you must have faith when He says, "No." You must say, "God, I believe that you know something that I don't know." I've prayed this prayer when God has told me "No" at different times; and I've just had to say, "God I know that You know something that I don't know. And I just believe in my heart that You are protecting me in some way—because You love me. Lord, thank you, thank you, thank you." Responding to God's "No" with faith will always be rewarded. Forcing the door will always cost you.

Seeing Glory in the "No"

Some of Jesus' dearest friends during His ministry on earth were Mary, Martha, and their brother Lazarus. They shared many good experiences and Jesus spent time with them in their home. As your read of their relationship in the scriptures, it seems that they are like family to Jesus. At one point, Lazarus becomes very sick, and Mary and Martha send word to Jesus to ask the Lord to come and heal their brother and His friend. This powerful story is found in John 11.

"Now a certain man was sick, Lazarus of Bethany. In the town of Mary and her sister, Martha. It was that Mary that anointed the Lord with fragrant oil and wiped his feet with her hair, who's brother Lazarus was sick. Therefore, the sisters went to him, 'Lord behold he whom you love. He is sick.' When Jesus heard that he said, 'This sickness is not unto death, but for the glory of God. That the son of God could be glorified through it.' Now, Jesus loved Martha and her sister, and Lazarus and when he heard that he was sick he stay two more days in the place where he was. And after this he said to his disciples, 'Let us go to Judea again.'" John 11:1-7 NKJV

Notice that Jesus, upon hearing of Lazarus being sick, does not rush over to heal His sick friend. Instead, He stays two more days and during that time Lazarus dies! Jesus knows this and even tells His disciples, "Lazarus is dead. And for your sakes, I'm glad I wasn't there, for now you will really believe." (John 11:14-15) Did you catch that?! "I'm glad I wasn't there"?! Now we know Jesus isn't sadistic, so what did He mean? Let's look at the story again.

By waiting two days Jesus is basically saying, "No" to Mary and Martha's request of Him to come and heal their brother. Jesus' motives and purpose is revealed when He says, "This sickness is not unto death, but for the glory of God. That the Son of God could be glorified through it." Jesus was setting up this situation for a demonstration of His glory. Mary and Martha couldn't understand it. And if this were you or I, we probably wouldn't understand it either.

Instead, we would think something like, "What possible good can come from you allowing my brother to die? I made a simple request. You said 'No', and now look at what's happened!!" Jesus eventually does come to them and does something beyond the scope of their reasoning—He raises Lazarus from the dead! In doing this He brings even greater glory to the situation. But too often, in all the emotions and trauma of these great tests to our faith—we don't see the glory in the "No."

Have you ever prayed for somebody who was sick and they died? I have and it can be a very dark hour of the soul as you look into the eyes of that widow or that weeping child. Questions swirl around in our mind as we try and sort it out. As a Christian, we must lay hold of a spirit of faith. Our trust must be in the One Who knows why—even when He doesn't tell us why. I had one such moment when I was a senior in high school. I had met a young girl named Shelley. She was bright and joyful and full of life. We became good friends and I had the privilege of leading her to Christ. In the spring of my senior year, I went with my church on a ministry trip. While I was away, Shelley and a friend were in a horrible car accident. The little car they were driving was demolished and almost unrecognizable. Shelley's friend, Virginia, was critically injured. Shelley's injuries were much worse. She suffered severe head trauma and was in a coma. When I returned home I went to the hospital again and again. Each time I came home from the hospital, I went into the church sanctuary and prayed. Every day after school, for almost three weeks, I went into the church and pleaded with God to raise her up and spare her life. The trauma to her brain was so great that she succumbed to death and passed into eternity. I will never forget the phone call from her parents telling me she was dead. For a seventeen year old, it was a very difficult time in my life. My trust and faith in God is what got me through that dark hour. I had prayed dozens of prayers and pleaded with God—interceding for a miracle. But He said, "No." I didn't understand it then, and I still don't now. But I have come to know this: we don't live by what we know, we live by what we believe.

The scripture tells us, "The just shall live by faith." (Romans 1:17) It does not say, "The just shall live by what he knows or understands." It also does not say, "The just shall live by what he feels." We cannot live by what we know because in this life there is too much that is beyond our comprehension or understanding. We cannot live by our feelings either because feelings and emotions are unstable, volatile, and unreliable. We must live our lives by faith—what we believe!

When Jesus finally makes it to Mary and Martha, they are distraught with grief over the death of their brother. Jesus tells them, "Your brother will rise again." (John 11:23) Then Jesus makes the following statement:

"Jesus said to her, "I am the resurrection and the life. He who believes in Me, though he may die, he shall live. And whoever lives and believes in Me shall never die. Do you believe this?"" John 11:25-26 NKJV

Jesus uses the word "believe" three times in His statement. What is He saying? Jesus is calling her to stand in faith. He has said, "No" to them and yet He still calls them to believe. She replies, "Yes, Lord, I believe." She responds to His call to faith. She takes her stand, not in the emotions of the moment nor in her limited understanding and knowledge. She plainly declares her faith in spite of Jesus' "No." And so must we.

There are times when God will say, "No" to you and you must take it in a spirit of faith. There will come a time when what you ask of the Lord is good and right and noble. And

He will say, "No." It is in that hour that you position yourself in faith. Do not trust your feelings. Do not rely on your experience or the wisdom of man. But stand in faith. Let an attitude of submission and trust grow in your heart and boldly confess with your mouth, "I trust you Lord! You are good! You will take what is meant for evil and turn it for good. In this difficult time strengthen me with Your grace and fortify my soul with faith. I believe Your word and Your promises. I don't rely on my experience or my feelings. Instead, I submit what I know and how I feel to the word of truth. I believe You are a good God, Who will turn this for good and display Your glory!!"

When the story of Lazarus concludes—it ends in a blaze of glory! Jesus said, "This sickness is not unto death, but for the glory of God. That the Son of God could be glorified through it." The ultimate goal of Christ when He says "No" is to work His glory into the situation. Too often our view of it all is clouded by our desires. While our desires may be noble, it is often something much more grand and powerful that God is after. We just can't see it.

I'm reminded of the story of a woman who lost her husband to disease. They both were fifty years old with lots of life left to live. Then he was diagnosed with the disease and within weeks he was gone. They had prayed and fasted, and then, he died. He was a born again believer, so he went home to heaven. That's the glorious hope we have, those that die in faith go to be with the Lord. And they are in heaven forevermore. But this doesn't take away from the fact that this was now a 50 year old widow who had lost her husband to a disease that she had prayed against and now he was no longer there. Where is the glory in that? Interestingly enough, one of this woman's life-long dreams was to be a missionary to Asia. At 50 years of age she entered into a one year training program, learned about surviving, ministering, and serving God in a foreign field. Her training complete, she went to Asia where she gave the remaining 30 years of her life to preaching the Gospel. As a result, 400 churches were planted. Tens of thousands of people were saved. All because God said, "No." Had her husband lived, she might not have pursued the call of God. But when God said, "No" to her, He was working for a much more glorious purpose. He used a loss and turned it into gain. He took a tragedy and turned it into His triumph. He brought glory out of His "No."

It requires faith to see the glory when you lose someone, or when sickness is there and it continues to go on. I continue to pray for my son to be healed from his deafness, but I also continue to look for the glory in his deafness until he would be healed. Part of that glory that I'm talking about is a class of people coming to the church every week for 14 weeks to be taught sign language by my wife. Many of those people, who do not know the Lord, heard the Gospel. We shared the gospel and our testimony with them. If my son was not deaf, that would not have happened. There are things of glory that an attitude of faith must see. It requires faith to see the glory in the loss, in the sickness, in the death. It takes an attitude of faith. And your spirit needs to say, "Lord, I know You are good, and I know that even though this is bad, I can see glory here. Open up my eyes and help me see Your glory in this situation." That is having faith when God says, "No."

What's Your Attitude?

When God says "No," we have a choice. We can get a bad attitude. We can get bitter. Or we can face all these things going on in our lives, and choose to respond with faith. Our confession should be, "God, I know You are good. I'm going to look for the glory in this. I believe you're protecting me somehow. And I choose to believe the best about you, about this situation, and about the glory that you are going to work through my life!" You must handle all of the "No's" with an attitude of faith. The faith response we have is based on God's word — the source of faith.

A Biblical Response When God Says "No"

Use these scriptures as declarations of faith when God says "No." Realize that He loves you and that He will work things out for your good and for His glory!

I commit my ways to You, Lord, and I trust You, knowing you will bring Your will to pass. Psalm 37:5

I will trust You at all times. I will pour out my heart to You and You will be a refuge to me. Psalm 62:8

I will not fear bad news because my heart is steadfast, trusting in the Lord. Psalm 112:7

I trust in the Lord with all my heart and I will not rely on my own understanding. In all my ways I will acknowledge Him and He will direct my path. Proverbs 3:5-6

I know that God causes everything to work together for my good because I love Him and I am called according to His purpose. Romans 8:28

I am convinced that nothing can ever separate me from God's love. Neither death nor life, neither angels nor demons, neither my fears for today nor my worries about tomorrow—not even the powers of hell can separate me from God's love. No power in the sky above or in the earth below—indeed, nothing in all creation will ever be able to separate me from the love of God that is revealed in Christ Jesus my Lord. Romans 8:38-39

I know that You can do everything, and that no purpose of Yours can be withheld from You. Job 42:2

The thoughts that You think towards me are thoughts of good and not evil, to give me a bright future and hope. When I call on You in prayer, You will listen to me. When I seek You I will find You, when I seek for You with all my heart. Jeremiah 29:11-13

I consider that the sufferings of this present time are not worthy to be compared with the glory which shall be revealed in me. Romans 8:18

For my light affliction, which is but for a moment, is working for me a far more exceeding and eternal weight of glory, and I do not look at the things which are seen, but at the things which are not seen. For the things which are seen from my human perspective are temporary, but the things which are seen from God's perspective are eternal. 2 Corinthians 4:17-18

My desire is that the name of the Lord Jesus Christ may be glorified in me, and I in Him, according to the grace of my God and the Lord Jesus Christ. 2 Thessalonians 1:12

My prayer for you is that you stand strong in faith—even when God says, "No." It is a struggle. I know. I've been there. And that's when faith matters most.

Chapter 6
When Faith needs Patience

"When God made his promise to Abraham, he backed it to the hilt, putting his own reputation on the line. He said, "I promise that I'll bless you with everything I have—bless and bless and bless!" Abraham stuck it out and got everything that had been promised to him."
Hebrews 6:13-15 THE MESSAGE

Our whole life is lived by faith. Isn't that what the scripture says? "The just shall live by faith." (Romans 1:17) Because of this, there are times in our lives when we really need to stir our faith, strengthen our faith, increase our faith, and build our faith. The Bible says to build yourself up in your most holy faith (Jude 20). All of these things are to be done. What is really important is to not lose your faith in what God wants to do, His motive for you, His desires for you, all of those things—not to lose any of that in the times when we need faith the most. In all of life's trials and tests, valleys and victories—we must keep a strong spirit of faith.

When I was growing up, we would go to the store or shopping mall and I would really want something I had seen at the store. Sometimes I'd be going to the store with my agenda in mind. We'd get in the car and I probably drove my dad crazy because I remember all the way to the store, I would be asking my dad about it. "Can I have this?" or "Can I have that?" My dad would sometimes give me a straight up "Yes" or "No". But the answer that drove me crazy was the reply, "We'll see." Now of course the "yes" was thrilling. "No" was a little disappointing, but at least I knew where he stood. But, "We'll see" was simply…excruciating! I have one question—what kind of an answer is "We'll see?!" I remember my mind racing. Am I going to able to get that toy when we get to the store? Am I being tortured by my dad? "We'll see." What does that mean? That answer was torture for a little kid. I hated that answer. Of course what's really great is now that I'm older and I have kids, I get to do that to them!

The "We'll see" answer helped me learn to wait. I'm not sure you could call it patience, but I learned to wait.

Sometimes God seems to say, "We'll see," and during those times He is often calling us to be patient.

One of the most challenging scriptures concerning our life of faith is found in the book of Hebrews. Hebrews 6:9-15 "But, beloved, we are confident of better things concerning you, yes, things that accompany salvation, though we speak in this manner. For God is not unjust to forget your work and labor of love which you have shown toward His name, in that you have ministered to the saints, and do minister. And we desire that each one of you show the same diligence to the full assurance of hope until the end, that you do not become sluggish, but imitate those who **through faith and patience inherit the promises**. For when God made a promise to Abraham, because He could swear by no one greater, He swore by Himself, saying, "Surely blessing I will bless you, and multiplying I will multiply you." And so, after he had patiently endured, he obtained the promise." (emphasis mine)

This passage is very clear. We inherit God's promises *through faith and patience.* It is not an either-or option, but both. You will not receive God's promises only through faith. Neither can you just wait only in patience. We receive His promises through faith AND patience. It's possible that when you hear the word "patience," you just can't wait till this chapter is over. But I want you to think about this principle. Learn from the word of God and allow it to challenge and change you.

Promise Delayed

All of us have promises we have received from God. The promise is given and then the wait begins. It is during that time of waiting that faith finds significance. Seasons of delay will prove what kind of faith you possess.

Every promise has a timer, a "set time" for it to be fulfilled. But when the time passes and days turn into weeks and weeks turn into months and months turn into years...we begin to wonder about the promise. I have actually said to God, "You know, I'm not getting any younger here! What's the hold up? Is it me? Have I failed You or done something that has disqualified me?" Question after question seems to roll through my mind trying to figure out the delay. During these times, you can become very hard and bitter or disillusioned. I have seen many people cave to anger and resentment over the delay of God's promise to them. In some cases, I have watched them throw away their very relationship with

God. They did not wait, they did not continue, they did not stick with it.

Impatience Rehab

When you get saved you buy into God's program of patience. I wish that godly character was something that you could rub the magic lamp three times and get it. Life is not like that. Patience is part of the package when you get saved. Hebrews 6:9 speaks of "things that accompany salvation." When you become a Christian you automatically get checked into God's impatience rehab program. He's trying to dry you out from your impatience. Impatience is such a weakness in our lives. In our 21st century world, we rarely have to wait for things. We can go online and order a book, pay for it, and within a few hours or days at the most, it is delivered right to our door! We can order a pizza and have it delivered to our door in 30 minutes or less! And if the pizza delivery guy is a moment late, we're on him for a free pizza!! All too often this transfers into our spiritual world. We want patience, but we want it now! We read a promise in the Scriptures and then whine about the time it takes to receive it! One thing is for sure, every promise has a process connected to it. Without patience for the process one can abort the promise!

I grew up in a pastor's home. There are many memories of people getting saved and lives transformed. I remember growing up hearing a story from my dad about a woman in our church in Missoula, Montana who had a kind of halfway house for drug addicts. It was the hippie movement and that generation had been introduced to LSD and heroin. Many young people experimented, got high, and tragically, got fried. One of the young men at this half-way house had so burned his brain out on drugs that when food was served to him at the table, he would just sit there staring at the plate. He had to be told to eat. Slowly, he would raise his hand, drag a fork off the table and clumsily feed himself—all the while staring with empty eyes. Many other addicts were getting clean the hard way. They would get into a room and shake violently, getting sick and feverish as they went through the ugly crucible of drying out from heroin. I made a promise to myself when I saw the wretchedness of the drug culture that I would never do drugs! I never did. All through high school I had several opportunities and never went into that world I saw so vividly as a boy.

Impatience, while not a narcotic, is still just as destructive and its consequences are even more devastating. The process for breaking free from impatience is not easy. You will have the shakes of frustration; the fever of "have it your way"; and the nausea of delay. But in order for you to receive the promises of God, patience must replace impatience and faith is the key to breaking free into confident waiting.

Life Imitates Faith

Scripture calls us to "not become sluggish [lazy], but *imitate* those who through faith and patience inherit the promises" (Hebrews 6:12 emphasis mine). The Message Bible says, "Don't drag your feet. *Be like those* who stay the course with committed faith and then get everything promised to them" (emphasis mine). The word *imitate* is taken from a word that means *to mimic*. The idea being that what is seen and heard is then mimicked or imitated. The faith that is being referred to is not of some human origin, but of that given by God to pursue and possess His promises. Faith here is not the content of faith—some sort of concept we acknowledge with the mind, but rather it is the attitude of faith—that which is received from God and grasped by us and gripped with tenacity. This is a summons to keep an attitude of faith in life and into death. To mimic the spirit of faith of those who have possessed the promises is to move forward in a faith that is like their faith. It is to mimic that faith, mirror that faith, reproduce that faith in you.

Ever since I was a kid, I have loved imitating people. Bugs Bunny, John Wayne, Jimmy Stewart, were just a few of the targets of my imitation. Part of our holy calling to faith is to imitate those who have lived great lives of faith. They are our heroes of faith—those who we see in the bible or those who have been examples in our lifetime. I'm speaking of the men and women who have demonstrated an amazing life of faith. All of them have not only demonstrated wonderful faith, but have combined their faith with patience.

The Call to Patience

One of the virtues that we are to imitate is found in Hebrews 6:12. Scripture warns us not to become lazy, and instead calls us to imitate those who through faith and patience inherit the promise. We imitate. We do what they did. It is a mandate to look at their example and take notes on patience. What can we learn from these examples? Here are a few important principles about the value God places on patience.

1. **To be patient is to share in the nature of God.**

   Romans 2:4 speaks of "…the riches of his good-ness, forbearance and longsuffering". Patience and longsuffering are the same. Go ahead, say it how you feel it. "Loooongsuffering." Because that's how it feels, right? Yet, this is a quality of God that we are supposed to live out in our life of faith. The value of patience is referred to when the word "riches" is used to describe it. Patience makes our faith richer. It makes the promise sweeter. Patience is the sweet marinade that soaks the faith-promise so that it becomes even better when we taste it! When we wait in faith and patience it also makes us sweeter as well.

2. **Patience is one of the qualities of a minister of God.**

   In 2 Corinthians 6:6 the apostle Paul declares, "I'm living my life by purity, by knowledge, by longsuffering [or patience], by kindness, by the Holy Spirit and by sincere love." Are you living your life by patience? Are you living your life by longsuf-fering? If you are a believer, you are a minister. You have a ministry that God wants you to fulfill and you must fulfill it through patience. Ministry involves people, needs, and destiny. These three have one thing in common—process. In order to handle the process of ministry you must minister with patience.

3. Patience is part of the Fruit of the Spirit.

You remember the list in Galatians 5:22. "But the Holy Spirit produces this kind of fruit in our lives: love, joy, peace, patience, kindness, goodness, faithfulness, gentleness, and self-control." What did Jesus do to the fig tree that wasn't bearing fruit? What happened? He cursed it. Now apply that principle to the Fruit of the Spirit. Jesus comes, inspects the plant in a believer's life and there is no fruit. No love, no joy, no peace, no patience...and that person wonders why it seems that he is striving and fighting against some invisible wall that is keeping him from his promise. That "wall" he is facing is the curse of lacking the fruit of the Spirit. Do you have the fruit?

4. Patience helps us walk worthy of our calling.

Ephesians 4:2 calls us to walk with "all lowliness and gentleness, with longsuffering, bearing with one another in love." But in the first verse he says, "I want you to walk worthy of the calling with which you were called." Patience is a part of that walk. It is a part of our calling. You are called to be a patient person. The inverse is also true. A person can walk unworthy of their calling by being impatient. This is why Saul lost his kingdom. He wasn't willing to wait for the prophet Samuel. Instead, he allowed the impulse of impatience to overwhelm him and he lost his kingdom as a result. It is why people everyday are throwing away their potential because they don't want to connect patience to their faith. They don't realize that in casting off patience, they inject weakness into their faith and over time that faith withers and dies and their calling is cast aside.

5. Patience is to be accompanied with joy.

The Bible says in Colossians 1:11, that you must be "strengthened with all might, according to His glorious power, for all patience and longsuffering with joy." Joy is what makes the wait easier. If we are to wait in our faith, why not enjoy the wait? Joy is our strength (Nehemiah 8:10). It even sustained

Jesus as He endured the cross (Hebrews 12:1-3). Over the years I have discovered that joy, as with all attitudes, is a choice. If you are going to wait, don't wait with tears. Wait in fun, laughter, and joy. The key to doing this is to remind yourself of why you're waiting. That is how Jesus could handle the cross with joy. He looked down through the ages and saw you! It all became worth it in that moment.

The Consequences of Impatience

It happens to all of us. We get tired of waiting and we try the shortcut—only to find out that what we thought was a shortcut turns out to actually take longer than if we would have waited patiently. When it comes to faith there are no shortcuts. Every promise of God has divine timing and kingdom goals to fulfill. We are not the time-keepers or goal-setters. All of these are in the hand of our God and we must follow the divine pattern or life can become very messy. Being impatient has consequences.

1. The problems that accompany self-effort.

Self-effort is our attempts to make things work outside of God's resources. Whether it's moving without His wisdom or blundering forward in the wrong timing, self-effort is nothing more than striving in our flesh. It happens when you get tired of waiting and you decide to "make things happen." This is usually our effort without God's involvement, which is a great definition for foolishness!! A host of problems await anyone who strives in self-effort. Like the person who tries to put something together without reading the directions, so we try to work our way through a challenge, only to discover the pieces left over. It doesn't work. Be patient for God's resources. Whether it's wisdom, finances, direction, or something else. Don't let impatience get the upper hand. Expectantly wait for His supply and then act.

2. Wasted time.

I saw a commercial once of a guy out for a fun day with the family on the lake. He's got his boat in tow and he is on his way to water ski heaven! The only problem, he's lost. Ignoring the GPS, he takes the "shortcut", and the next picture you see is of the dusty SUV towing an even dustier boat out in the middle of the desert!! If he would have only listened to the directions and followed them he could have been wake boarding by then! He wasted his time by not being patient with the directions given. How many of us have wasted time because we would not wait. We take a "shortcut" only to discover that we have to go back, retrace our steps, and in the end it is longer than if we would have been patient.

3. Lost reward.

Elisha's servant, Gehazi, is a powerful illustration of what happens when you are impatient. Gehazi was chosen to be the successor to Elisha. He was the servant of the prophet and by tradition stood to receive the training and eventually the ministry of his mentor. But when confronted with the temptation to make something happen, he chose not to wait for the reward of patience, but instead chose his own plan for success and reward. As a result, he traded the reward for a curse and died a leper. It's possible that even your life and all the plans that you lay out there comes under a curse because you're not willing to wait. You trade God's plan for a plan of your own— your bulleted list, your timeline, and your calendar.

If you don't submit to the process and plan of God, you run the risk of losing your reward. Waiting cancels wasting. Patience empowers faith to cash in on God's promises. Patience is what brings you to the fulfillment of the faith-promise.

Powerful Keys For Waiting In Faith

Waiting in faith is not accidental it is intentional. Like it or not you will wait for promises to be fulfilled. In that moment there must be a decisive conviction. "I'm going to believe God. I am going to stand here and wait, but I'm going to wait in faith." Waiting in faith can become easier when we practice these keys while we wait.

1. Never assume God is not working.

It's important for you to get this in your heart. I realize that some of you are waiting for that unsaved spouse to get saved. Don't assume God is not working. I get why you may feel the way you do. I mean, you just look at the guy and he is a post with clothes on. There is no spiritual life evident at all—not even a flicker of spiritual interest! Some of you are waiting for that particular change of events or for that promise to be fulfilled or that particular desire to be met. And all of a sudden you're just thinking, "Hello! God!" You are just convinced that God saw a vacation deal He couldn't miss and He's out having fun somewhere. But the scripture says, "Faithful is He who called you who also will do it." (1 Thessalonians 5:24 NKJV) The idea in that scripture is not only that He will do it, but that He is doing it until it is done. It means that God is at work. Working until it is finished. What did Jesus do on the cross? What were His words right before He died? He said, "It is finished." What was He doing all the way up until that moment? Working. And by the way 30 years of that time He was working and nobody saw Him, nobody knew Him, most of the world didn't even know He existed. He didn't even start His ministry until He was 30 years old. So He had 30 years of waiting. Never assume God is not working. God is working. Just because you don't see evidence does not mean there is no activity. I planted grass at my house one time and I was watering it and caring for it. And my kids were constantly asking, "When is the grass coming up?" and I told them, "Well it just takes time." And you know what? Things were happening. Things were happening underneath that soil and with that seed. You couldn't see it. But several days later there were sprouts that became little green signals that something is happening, but until that moment you don't see anything. Just because you don't see the evidence doesn't mean there is no activity.

2. Stay convinced of the perfect timing of God.

God has an amazing sense of timing. It's just unbelievable. And every time we are sure that there is no progress with the promise, we need to be convinced in our mind that God has got an appointment for His promise and He is never late for His appointments. He is always perfectly on time. Your calendar needs to be submitted to His calendar so that what is on His calendar gets transferred to yours. Every piece of fruit has a time when it is to be eaten. And it is the same way with God's process in your life. Have you ever had a piece of fruit and it's a little early and you're puckering up with the sourness? Or have you eaten a piece of fruit and it's a little late? "Oh! Where is the expiration date on this thing?" And you're over at the sink spitting it out. The cool thing about God is that when He gives you the fruit of the promise and you get that fruit from Him, it is perfect every time. If succulence in fruit could be gauged down to the very moment—that is the kind of thing God does with His promises. He brings it to you, right when it is perfectly ripe, you'll sink your teeth in, and say, "That's what I'm talking about!!" Stay convinced that God's promise is on time. Don't let yourself, don't let your friends, don't let the pressures of other people, don't let your own agenda, don't let the devil come in and tell you that God has forgotten about you.

The Bible says in Romans 4:21: "*I am fully convinced that what He has promised He is also able to perform.*" God keeps His appointments. 2 Timothy 1:12 "*For this reason I also suffer these things; nevertheless I am not ashamed, for I know whom I have believed and am persuaded that He is able to keep what I have committed to Him until that Day.*" He's going to keep His appointment with you.

3. Ask for grace to wait.

I believe that God gives grace for you to have patience. 1 Peter 4:10 speaks of "the manifold grace of God". That word 'manifold' there means many-colored or multifaceted. The idea is *many facets.* Like a diamond that displays its beauty and splendor with the facets of the cut, so grace has many facets that apply to different areas of our lives. Anybody need grace to resist temptation? God's got grace for that. God has grace for overcoming strongholds in your life. God has grace for dealing with habits that you have struggled with for years. And He also has grace for patience. When you come to God and say, "I need grace for patience." Ask Him. The Bible says in Hebrews 4:16 "come boldly to the throne of grace." Why do you do that? "To find grace and mercy to help in time of need." Ask for grace to wait. Say, "God give me grace to wait in faith," and He will give it to you.

4. Be consistently faithful.

You know those 30 years Jesus waited until His manifestation? What was He doing? Showing His faithfulness. The forty years Moses was in the wilderness before he became a deliverer, what was he doing? Showing his faithfulness. The 120 years that Noah kept falling trees and carving them out and building a boat so that he could be saved from the flood. What is that called? Faithfulness. Patience is what turns faith into faithfulness. Being consistent in your faith is what turns faith into faithfulness. Anyone can have a "flash of faith" that comes in the moment of excitement and promise. It takes a faithful person to consistently do the right things, over a period of time, to inherit the promise.

5. Determine to grow.

One of the reasons you are in the "holding pattern" of waiting is because God wants you to grow. He is working on your character. The best response you could give God is to make up your mind, "I'm going to change. I'm going to grow and improve. The way I've been is not like me. I'm going to become better." If you have ever tried to get into shape, you have probably heard the workout proverb: "No pain, no gain!" Too often we forget that patience is often translated *longsuffering*. This is a compound word—one word from two. The first is the word *long* – the patience part of the word. The second part of the word—*suffering*—is the pain part of the word. This is why patience is so unpopular. But if you are willing to endure, even when it's painful, you will grow. Just as your body loses weight, trims down, and tones up when you work out. So your soul gets into shape when you wait in faith. Faith makes the decision to grow during the waiting. Faith makes the wait worth it.

6. Wait for a word before you act.

Too many people, after waiting for a time, take action without hearing a clear word from God. Jesus said, "Man shall not live by bread alone, but by every word that proceeds from the mouth of God." (Matthew 4:4 NKJV) This keeps you from taking matters into your own hands. Too often people move out of frustration, or pressure, or some other circumstance. There are far too many Christians today who are making decisions without so much as a prayer, let alone an answer! If the just are to live by faith, and faith comes by hearing a word from God, then we must have a revolution in how we wait! We must wait until we hear, then move on the word. Moses waited in the wilderness until a word from God altered his life at the burning bush, and on that word from God, a deliverer emerged from the wilderness! Peter essentially disqualified himself when he denied Christ, yet the words "feed my sheep" changed the man from dismal denier to powerful preacher and whose first altar call resulted in 3,000 salvations on the day of Pentecost!! Faith needs patience because faith needs a word to be activated. Wait for the word and faith will be released. Once you receive the word—act on it!!

7. Never give up.

I was with a group of students when I was in college talking to a very respected minister named Leonard Fox. He had experience and wisdom and, seeking insight for fruitful ministry, the students asked him, "How in the world have you lasted so long in the ministry?" And he said, "Well, I can sum it all up in just three words." We were shocked that the mystery could be so simple. He just looked at us and said, "Never give up. It's that simple. Just never give up." You know, those three words have saved me many times. All of us will face the challenge when our faith must have patience. During the wait, no matter how long it drags on, no matter how powerful the pressure or how searing the stress— NEVER GIVE UP!! When faith needs patience we must have this commitment.

Most people reading this book hate to wait. Waiting is loathed—detested. Can I recommend something radical? Fall in love with patience. Learn to love the process that God has you in. Impatience has serious consequences. Don't cut corners. Don't take the shortcut. It's a trap to get you to take matters into your own hands and undermine God's process for your promise. Just as it takes faith to believe the promise, it also takes patience to possess the promise. Please wait for it. Be faith-filled and patient. If you do, you will join the great cloud of witnesses who "through faith and patience received the promises."

Chapter 7
Keeping Faith When You Fail

"The godly may trip seven times, but they will get up again."
Proverbs 24:16a NLT

I have read the bible many times and have studied it for decades, yet the exploits of the men and women of faith never cease to amaze me. Time after time these great heroes of faith inspire me with their exploits and demonstrations of great faith. Hebrews 11:1-2 says, *"Now faith is the substance of things hoped for, the evidence of things not seen. <u>For by it the elders obtained a good testimony</u>."* The elders are those who have gone on before us in faith. 1 Corinthians 10:6 tells us that "all these things became our examples." The emphasis of the scriptures is that these "elders", our predecessors in faith, are our examples. From their lives of faith we draw lessons of faith.

Think for a moment of their names—Abraham, Sarah, Joseph, Moses, Miriam, Ruth, David, Peter, Paul, and so on. All of us who have read their stories would freely admit they were people of tremendous faith. Yet, faith is not all that they had in common. There is something else they all had in common that we share with them. What is it? Failure. Every one of them failed at some point in their life. And if you would join me in a moment of true confessions: We all have failed. We know what it is to fail. But the question is what are you going to do when failure occurs in your life?

I don't know of any human being who wants to fail or be a failure. Studies throughout all of humanity have proven that one of our core fears is the fear of failure. This is why it is so brutal when you do fail. You fail. You blow it. You mess up. You do something you shouldn't have done. You miss the mark. You fail. What are you going to do at that moment of realization? Will you crumble under the failure? Will you allow it cripple you?

Faith matters most when you are confronted with your failures. Pressing through the failure and into fulfilling your destiny is a matter of faith. People are not defined by their success. People are defined by their failures and how they handle them. All those people I just listed failed. They didn't fail just once or twice, but over and over again. What made them great are not all their successes. What makes them great is how they handled failures and they kept going in faith. That is why Hebrews 11 says, "by this, the elders [our predecessors] obtained a good testimony." It's been said that you can't have a testimony without a test. The key for having a good testimony is to be able to make it through your failures in a spirit of faith.

Righteousness is not the Absence of Failure

Proverbs 24:16 "For a righteous man may fall seven times and rise again, but the wicked shall fall by calamity." Notice that this scripture does not say that the righteous will not face calamity. It is saying that the righteous will rise from it and move forward. What overwhelms the wicked is their inability to rise out from the calamity and move forward in faith. The righteous person gets up in a spirit of faith and moves past the calamity, past the failure, and past the hard experience. That's the difference. Evil people will perish in the calamity, but the righteous overcome failure with faith.

Who Are Some Failures in the Bible?

- Adam & Eve failed to obey God.

- Cain failed to love his brother & resist sin.

- Joseph's brothers failed to overcome jealousy.

- Israel failed to believe God for victory over their enemies.

- Moses failed to obey God and speak to the rock.

- Israel failed to drive out their enemies.

- Saul failed to overcome his insecurities.

- David failed to follow God's pattern of handling the Ark of the Covenant.

- David failed morally with Bathsheba.

- David failed to obey the 6th Commandment (You shall not murder).

- David failed as a parent.

- David failed as a Commander-In-Chief (numbered the fighting men).

- Solomon failed to honor the marriage covenant.

- Peter failed when he rebuked the Lord.

- Peter failed when he forsook the Lord.

- Peter failed when he denied the Lord.

- Judas failed when he betrayed the Lord.

- Thomas failed when he did not believe.

- Ananias & Sapphira failed when they lied to the Holy Spirit.
- The early church failed when they neglected the widows.
- John Mark failed when he turned back on his commitment.
- Demas failed when he forsook Paul for the world.
- Hymenaeus and Alexander failed concerning the faith and a pure conscience.
- Onesimus failed his employer.
- The church in Laodicea failed Jesus through lukewarmness.

Now that's the short list. Allow me to make a shocking statement: The Bible is a book of failure. Scripture is filled with people who have failed over and over again.

What Is Failure?

The word *fail* means:

- To lose strength; to fade; or stop functioning.
- To fall short; to be or become absent or inadequate; unsuccessful.
- To disappoint expectations or trust.

- To be deficient in – Lack
- To leave undone – Neglect

All of us have done one or more of these things. How will you handle your failure? Will you allow it to define your life or will you face your failures with faith and press through them?

How Does Faith Define Failure?

Failures are the costly lessons we learn to achieve success! When I was a kid and I did something to fail and my dad would say, "Son, I'm going to teach you a lesson." Being interpreted, that means my backside is going to get whupped. Now, in life you can be taught a lesson. You will fail. But there is a difference between being taught a lesson and *learning the lesson*. Learning the lesson is our part. Being taught the lesson is God's part. He wants to teach us the lesson, but we need to be able to learn the lesson or guess what? You are going to get taught the lesson again.

While reading an article, I came across the Rules for Being Human. They are:

Rule #1 – You will learn lessons.

Rule #2 – There are no mistakes only lessons

Rule #3 – A lesson is repeated until it is learned.

Rule #4 – If you don't learn the easy lessons, they get harder (Pain is the one way the universe gets your attention). How many of you laid your hand on the stove just because you were curious? Why don't you do that anymore? You learned your lesson. Why? Because it hurt!!

Rule #5 – You'll know you've learned a lesson when your actions change.[1]

Failure Is Not...

All of us are keenly aware of what our failures are. But even more important is understanding of what failure is not. Many of us have wrong concepts of failure. These concepts affect our faith. They limit our perspective and hinder our faith. When our faith is hindered, our destiny is hindered.

Failure Is Not:

1. Avoidable[2] – every person will fail at something in life. Do all that you can do to plan for success, and you will still not be able to avoid failure. I have two words for you. Apollo 13. The smartest men in the world

putting together a team to go to the moon. We are the only nation in the history of the world that has ever put someone on the moon. We should have it down. Yet everyone remembers the phrase, "Houston, we have a problem." Failure is just not avoidable. They thought they'd planned for everything. In spite of all your planning and preparation you will fail. Every person will fail at something in his or her life. Failure is unavoidable.

2. An event[3] – failure and success are aspects of our journey. When a person gets an F on a test it doesn't mean you failed a one-time event. The F shows that you neglected the process leading up to the test. Success is not an event—neither is failure. Failure happened in all the time when you didn't do your studying leading up to the test. I got my F from playing basketball instead of studying.

3. Objective[4] – it is true that only you can really label what you do as a failure. Failure is often highly sub-jective. You have all these personal expectations you put on yourself. When you don't hit the mark or you

fall short or you disappoint or you're unsuccessful, you come down hard on yourself. You have failed. What you don't realize is the "failure" is subjective. Really the only person that can label you as a failure is yourself. Faith will not think that way.

4. The enemy[5] – people who see failure as the enemy are captive to those who conquer it. Don't be afraid of failure, but embrace your failures and realize that they are opportunities to learn and grow. This is the response of faith. Faith has the power to turn failure from foe to friend.

5. Irreversible[6] – mistakes and failures are not irreversible. John Maxwell says, "Every event—whether good or bad—is one step in the process of living." If you fail, it's okay. You can make up for it. Faith boldly declares that failure is not the end. It faces the problem of failure and resolves it with the positive choice to change it—reverse it.

6. A stigma[7] (a mark against you.) – the novel, The Scarlet Letter revolves around a woman who failed

morally and was required to wear a red A on her clothing that stood for *adulteress.* She was to wear it everywhere she went, marking her for her failure. Your mistakes are not some scarlet letter you are cursed with. Some of us approach failure as if it was the mark of the Beast and now you are stamped and doomed. You're not. The late Senator Sam Ervin Jr. said, "Defeat may serve as well as victory to shake the soul and let the glory out." I've learned a lot from my own defeats and we need to deal with our defeats in faith. When you make mistakes, don't let them get you down. Don't think of them as stigmas.[8] God is better than that. Come on. Greater is He that is in you than your mistakes. Make each failure a step to success. That's how faith handles it.

7. Final[9] – there are many huge failures that look like the deathblow to our future. We must stand in faith, believing that those failures or blunders can be changed and actually be stepping-stones to our future. How many of you remember the soft drink "New Coke?" After a 20 year market decline to rival Pepsi, the Coca-Cola corporation decided to change

the time tested formula and market it as "New Coke." The decision proved a disaster and lasted a whopping 79 days and cost the Coca-Cola company a dizzying $100 million!! But this failure was not final. Instead, Coca-Cola reversed its position and announced the return of "Coca-Cola Classic." The change actually made the company stronger in the end.[10] Faith will not allow failure to be final. Instead faith will cause us to believe in the possibilities. Something that often gives birth to creativity and new perspective. When faith confronts failure it removes "final" from the equation. Faith gives us the belief to try again.

Failing *Forward*

John Maxwell gives these two opposite approaches to failure: Reacting or Responding. Are we to react to life's problems? No, we are to respond to them. Failing Backward is reacting. Failing *Forward* is responding.

Failing Backward	*Failing Forward*
• Blaming others	• Taking responsibility
• Repeating the same mistakes	• Learning from each mistake
• Expecting to never fail again	• Knowing failure is a part of progress
• Expecting to continually fail	• Maintaining a positive attitude
• Accepting tradition blindly	• Challenging outdated assumptions
• Being limited by past mistakes	• Taking new risks
• Thinking "I am a failure."	• Believing something didn't work
• Quitting	• Persevering[11]

Faith handles failure by moving forward. To slide back into a limited life because of failure is the result of handling failure without faith. When faith matters most is when, in the spirit of faith, you pick yourself out of the dirt of failure and dust yourself off from the muck of faltering. It is in that moment of rising again in faith that your righteous destiny is removed from jeopardy.

Overcoming Failure With Faith

1. Faith takes the U out of failure.

See, you need to stop telling yourself: I am a failure. The truth is you may have failed at something. You must handle this aggressively. It may seem a little awkward at first, but tell yourself, "I'm not a failure. I failed at doing something." There's a big difference.

Every genius could have been a failure. Wolfgang Mozart was told by Emperor Ferdinand that his opera *The Marriage of Figaro* was "far too noisy" and contained "far too many notes." Vincent Van Gogh, whose painting *Snow* set records for the sums of money they bring at auction, sold only one painting in his lifetime. Thomas Edison, the most prolific inventor in history, it took him over a thousand tries to invent the light bulb. Over a thousand tries. Someone even asked him one time, "Mr. Edison do you ever get discouraged with all those failures trying to invent the light bulb?" And he said, "No, I really don't really think of it like that. I just I learned 1000 ways not to make a light bulb." And

Albert Einstein was told by a Munich schoolmaster that he would "never amount to much."[12]

Just think if all these people would have taken the advice or the experiences of people in their life. And yet today we think that they are incredible. Why? Was history simply kind to them or was it something more? It was much more. They would not allow failure to overcome them or define them. You too must not allow your times of failure to relegate you to a life of failure. Stand up in faith and seize failure by the collar and show it to its place!

Don't personalize your failure. Make sure that your failure doesn't make you a failure. Believe in what God has for you. Greater is He that is in you than your failures. If you believe failing makes you a failure, you will never do anything with your life. You will always be bound in fear. And that fear is a result of you believing that you are a failure, instead of believing that you failed. Think of it this way: If you believe that failure makes you a failure you become trapped in the *Fear Cycle*.[13] (also in John Maxwell's book *Failing Forward*). If you have a fear of failure, then you will be stuck in a life of inaction. You will never try anything, you will never do anything. You can be so afraid of failure you will never try. And of course that inaction reinforces the inexperience that we have. And so we don't get any experience because we don't do anything. So we stay inexperienced. Our lack of experience in turn produces in us inability and so we stay in a lack of ability and become stuck in our inability. Feeling unable reinforces fear, which produces more inaction. And the cycle goes on and on. You need to take the U out of failure. Do not assume you are a failure just because you fail.

2. Faith will admit mistakes (failures).

This is also known as taking responsibility for your actions. I read recently hilarious explanations of why people get in accidents. They get in an accident and write it down as to what happened.

Drivers explanation for auto accidents in which they were involved:[14]

- "As I reached an intersection, a hedge sprang up, obscuring my vision."
- "An invisible car came out of nowhere, struck my car, and vanished."
- "The telephone pole was approaching fast. I attempted to swerve out of its path when it struck my front end."
- "The indirect cause of this accident was a little guy in a small car with a big mouth."
- "I had been driving my car for four years when I fell asleep at the wheel and had an accident."
- "I was on the way to the doctor's with rear-end trouble when my universal joint gave way, causing me to have an accident."

- "To avoid hitting the bumper of the car in front, I struck the pedestrian."
- "I was coming home, pulled into the wrong driveway, and hit a tree I did not have."
- "I was just keeping up with the cars behind me."
- "The pedestrian had no idea which direction to run, so I ran over him."
- "The guy was all over the road, and I had to swerve a number of times before hitting him."
- "I pulled away at the side of the road, glanced at my mother-in-law, and headed over an embankment."

We come up with the funniest explanations of why we do the things we do. We often fall into the trap of blame shifting. We just need to say, "I made a mistake. I blew it. I failed." We must accept responsibility for our failures. This is very critical if you want to move out of failure.

At first, accepting responsibility for failure appears to erode our faith—not build it. But the truth is that accepting responsibility for failure is an incredible act of faith. It takes faith to look at reality—then change. Any bump on a log can stay the same. It takes powerful faith to admit you blew it and then change it!

I have learned this – The person who will not admit his mistake is acting out of pride. It's all about pride. Straight up and flat out that is what it is. The person who doesn't admit mistakes or failure is proud. Pride will keep a person from changing. Pride is a prison. It will become a jail of failure. As long as a person continues in pride they will have trouble and continued failures. Scripture says, "Pride precedes a disaster, and an arrogant attitude precedes a fall." (Proverbs 16:18 GW) As long as a person is too proud to admit failure, they will feed weakness into their faith and remain imprisoned in failure.

Someone summarized this well when they joked, "If you could kick the person responsible for most of your troubles, you wouldn't be able to sit down for weeks!"

3. **Faith will not allow failure to become a mind-set.**

You must not think of yourself as a failure. It must not define who you are. It cannot define your future. Certainly, do not allow it to define your potential. Failure does none of those things unless failure becomes a mind-set. Then, all of those things will happen. The Bible tells us that, "As he thinks in his heart, so is he..." (Proverbs 23:7 NKJV) We are what we think. Much of our life is a product of our thinking. Faith must fill our minds and hearts when we fail. It's not easy, but it is necessary. Otherwise we shrivel into a life marked by failure thinking. We must have a faith mind-set.

Jesus faced his share of trials and failures. Opposition was often "in his face." His critics and enemies were usually plotting his death or some other devious resistance. Yet, it was Jesus who said, "With God nothing is impossible." What an attitude! He did not allow His mindset to become negative or cynical. Instead, He maintained faith in His Father and lived out that faith as an example for us.

4. Faith will put past failures behind you and move you on.

Think of it this way: There are people who have had it better than you and done worse. There are people who have had it worse than you and have done better. Circumstances really don't have anything to do with it—it's about what's inside.

Look at David. He committed murder and adultery. He wasn't that great of a father to his kids. He failed to handle the Ark of the Covenant properly. There are many different ways that he failed. The amazing characteristic of David was that, even though he failed, he did not allow it to define his future. He kept moving on. Paul said, "Forgetting those things which are behind and looking forward to those things which are ahead, I press on." (Philippians 3:13)

You have failed. You have had those times in life when you have really blown it. But let's press on. Let's get on with it. Let's learn our lesson and move on. No matter how bad your past is or how tragic life has been, remember that your life now is about *your future!* Faith looks forward. It spies out your potential and sees greatness. Faith observes life's failures as experience and wisdom. Those mistakes were lessons and now we will do better! It's all about your spirit of faith.

5. Faith will change the reason for the failure and grow.

There is a saying, "It's what you do after you get back up that counts." Faith will admit its mistakes. It will look at the failure and ask, "Why did that happen?" A faith response to failure seeks to improve, and when a weakness or flaw is found, a faith attitude will address it, change it and grow. Faith handles it that way. David is never seen committing adultery again. David never murders anyone else again. Think of that. Did Peter ever deny the Lord Jesus again? Do you think he had opportunity to? Absolutely. In Acts 3 Peter was told, "You are going to go to jail if you don't stop preaching Jesus." He could have shrunk back. The easy way out would have been to give up and give in—to deny his calling and mandate to be a witness. But instead he said, "No, I failed there before and I'm not doing that again. I will preach Jesus until the day I die! Throw me in jail! Handcuff me!!" Peter preached Jesus anyway. Why? Because he learned from his failure and grew.

Scripture tells us, "Though a righteous man falls seven times—he rises again." (Proverbs 24:16) Another way to say it is, "It's what you do after you get back up that counts." Handling failures with faith will cause you to rise again. After it feels as though failure has killed you, your resurrection to promise will come only as you "faith it" up and out of the tomb of failures past. You will rise in faith and be changed. Growth will be yours. New wisdom and understanding will be found. That which sought to limit you will become an opportunity for enlargement, if you handle it with faith.

Handling Your Failure

I think that we need to understand that failure is a reality of life. You and I can list many failing points in our lives. Here's the issue: Are you going to approach the failures in your life in a spirit of faith? Or are you going to allow them to define you? Are you going to let it become an inside job, or define your potential and your future? Hopefully you are saying, "No! I'm not going to let that happen. I'm going to stand in faith and believe that my God is greater than any failure that I could have experienced. I believe that the potential that it is in me can still be released even though I've failed!" Even if you may have limited your potential in some way with an attitude of unbelief or an attitude of failure, God can release you from that whole limitation, just by imparting into you a spirit of faith. Receive faith today and activate it by saying, "I will look at this failure as an opportunity to grow, and *I am going to grow*! I'm going to change what needs to be changed and I'm going to move on. I'm going to be better when the day is over." This spirit of faith will handle failure in a positive and powerful way.

What areas of your life do you need to evaluate? Is there a consistent failing point in your life? Take time to evaluate and then write down the areas that need to be addressed. You may need some advice or counsel. Instead of becoming discouraged or disillusioned with your failure, ask God for an infusion of faith to deal with it properly. He will give it to you. God is for your success. He is your Biggest Fan and He wants to help you through your failures. After all, when you fail is when your faith matters most!

Chapter 8
Facing Famine With Faith

"And God will generously provide all you need. Then you will always have everything you need and plenty left over to share with others."
2 Corinthians 9:8 NLT

As I write this book, my nation is in a great period of famine. It's a time of economic famine, spiritual famine, moral famine, a famine of leadership, and a famine of wisdom. Many cultures of the world understand famine on another level—where lack of water, food, nutrition, health care, or shelter are all affected. The bible speaks of times of famine as well. The patriarch Isaac experienced a famine, as did his father Abraham. During his season of famine, the bible tells us, "Isaac sowed in that land, and reaped in that same year a hundred more times grain than he had planted, for the Lord blessed him. The man began to prosper, and continued prospering until he became very prosperous." (Genesis 26:12-13). What was the key that enabled Isaac to come through famine with the blessing of the Lord? I believe the key for Isaac was that he sowed in faith, responding to God's word to him. He sowed in faith and God prospered him.

Some of you reading this book may struggle with the concept of prosperity or that God wants His people prosperous. While there are a few people who have become imbalanced and extreme with this truth, it does not invalidate the bible's clear doctrine that God wants to bless His people and prosper them. I urge you not to over react to erroneous teaching and throw out the wholesome balanced perspective of prosperity for a purpose, simply because of the errors of others. Prosperity is very clear in Genesis 26:13 — it's mentioned three times in one verse! Its use is even more powerful when you understand the context. Isaac prospered in a time of famine!!

Don't Go Down To Egypt

As Isaac watches, the effects of famine begin to become evident. Wells dry up. The ground becomes dry in the property adjoining his. Cattle in his neighbor's field are bellowing for food and water. Some are probably collapsing and dying—their carcasses becoming food for the vultures. Imagine the urge in Isaac to go to a place of provision. After all, his father Abraham did it. And in the midst of this calamity and trial God tells him, "Do not go down to Egypt, but do as I tell you." (Genesis 26:2 NLT) God speaks clearly to Isaac to stay and not look for his source elsewhere. Because of this word, Isaac's faith is stirred and he faces his time of famine with faith.

Egypt is a symbol of the world's economic system. The world has its own way of handling money and possessions. What's important is that we recognize the world's way of resources is flawed and doomed for failure. God knows this and in His wisdom He warns Isaac to "do as I tell you." In this instruction God is calling Isaac to follow God's economy, which is based on faith and giving. He forbids Isaac to follow the world's economy, which is based on fear and greed. Isaac followed God's economy and was blessed and prosperous.

What Is A Famine?

The term *famine* literally means *a scarcity of food*. It can also mean financial hard times. Another definition is a lack of supply for your needs. I have heard famine described as prosperity on pause. It has also been spoken of as financial leanness and want.

During a particular tight time in our lives, my wife and I had a mini-van that died with a failed transmission. The other car we had was gasping its last breath of existence, while the one good vehicle we had suddenly died on my wife in the store parking lot. No lights, no power, no action. Dead. It is in those moments of frustration that you question God. Thoughts like, "What's going on here?! I am a giver and I'm doing my best to be a good manager of the resources God has given me. What is the problem?!!!" Now if that were not enough, there were about three or four other urgent needs we had, and now we had to make some choices. In a nutshell, God came through for us and blessed us with solutions that were beyond our resources. In the end it turned out for good. But while in the midst of it, we became very aware of the absolute necessity to handle our little "famine" with faith.

Why Are We Allowed To Go Through Famine?

The bible gives us some astonishingly clear reasons why people experience famine. Deuteronomy 8:1-20 *"Every commandment which I command you today you must be careful to observe, that you may live and multiply, and go in and possess the land of which the LORD swore to your fathers. And you shall remember that the LORD your God led you all the way these forty years in the wilderness, to humble you and test you, to know what was in your heart, whether you would keep His commandments or not. So He humbled you, allowed you to hunger, and fed you with manna which you did not know nor did your fathers know, that He might make you know that man shall not live by bread alone; but man lives by every word that proceeds from the mouth of the LORD. Your garments did not wear out on you, nor did your foot swell these forty years. You should know in your heart that as a man chastens his son, so the LORD your God chastens you. Therefore you shall keep the commandments of the LORD your God, to walk in His ways and to fear Him. For the LORD your God is bringing you into a good land, a land of brooks of water, of fountains and springs, that flow out of valleys and hills; a land of wheat and barley, of vines and fig trees and pomegranates, a land of olive oil and honey; a*

*land in which you will eat bread without scarcity, in which
you will lack nothing; a land whose stones are iron and out
of whose hills you can dig copper. When you have eaten and
are full, then you shall bless the* LORD *your God for the good
land which He has given you. "Beware that you do not forget
the* LORD *your God by not keeping His commandments, His
judgments, and His statutes which I command you today,
lest—when you have eaten and are full, and have built beau-
tiful houses and dwell in them; and when your herds and
your flocks multiply, and your silver and your gold are multiplied, and all that you have is multiplied; when your heart
is lifted up, and you forget the* LORD *your God who brought
you out of the land of Egypt, from the house of bondage; who
led you through that great and terrible wilderness, in which
were fiery serpents and scorpions and thirsty land where
there was no water; who brought water for you out of the
flinty rock; who fed you in the wilderness with manna, which
your fathers did not know, that He might humble you and
that He might test you, to do you good in the end— then you
say in your heart, 'My power and the might of my hand have
gained me this wealth.' And you shall remember the* LORD
*your God, for it is He who gives you power to get wealth,
that He may establish His covenant which He swore to your*

fathers, as it is this day. Then it shall be, if you by any means forget the LORD your God, and follow other gods, and serve them and worship them, I testify against you this day that you shall surely perish. As the nations which the LORD destroys before you, so you shall perish, because you would not be obedient to the voice of the LORD your God."

This passage of Scripture is pretty clear as to God's motives. When God allows famine, or a time when we are challenged with lack, there are specific reasons why He allows it.

1. A consequence of disobedience.

Deuteronomy 8:1 says, "Every commandment which I command you today you must be careful to observe..." There are clear mandates that God gives us for our lives and when we disobey them there are consequences. The Scripture has commands, not suggestions. They are God's requirements for living our lives. When we follow His commands there is blessing that comes with obedience. When we ignore His commands or live for ourselves, there are consequences that come as a result of disobedience. One of the consequences for disobedience is lack or famine.

2. To cause us to remember the Lord.

The Scripture says, *"And you shall remember that the LORD your God led you all the way these forty years in the wilderness."* All too often we become forgetful that the Lord is our Source. He is the One Who supplies all our needs and gives us all we need for life. Without Him we can do nothing! In our self-centered and self-absorbed culture there is a tendency for us to forget that all we have and all we are, as believers, is because of the Lord and what He has done for us. When we stray into the place of selfishness, God will allow famine to bring us up short and remind us that everything comes from Him. Deuteronomy 8 later calls to us, *"Beware that you do not forget the LORD your God... then you say in your heart, 'My power and the might of my hand have gained me this wealth.'"* It is very important that we keep our perspective right and remember the Lord is our source!

3. To humble us and to test us.

"And you shall remember that the LORD your God led you all the way these forty years in the wil-

derness, to humble you and test you, to know what was in your heart, whether you would keep His commandments or not. So He humbled you, allowed you to hunger…" (Deuteronomy 8:2-3a)

Famine is sometimes allowed to test us and humble us. As previously mentioned self-centeredness is a hindrance and a problem many people must deal with. God will allow famine to humble us. James 4:6 says, "God resists the proud, but gives grace to the humble." And later, in verse 10, it says, "Humble yourselves in the sight of the Lord and He will lift you up." I believe it is much better for us if we *humble ourselves* than if we are *humbled by the Lord.* The former is our choice and the latter is chosen for us and worked into us, often more severely than if we had chosen to humble ourselves. Pride is the central theme of sin and was at the core of the original sin of Lucifer (Isaiah 14). When we become ensnared in pride we are only freed through humility. God will allow famine to deal with our pride and work a humble spirit into us.

Famine also tests us and proves what is in our hearts. If we are arrogant or proud, when famine comes, we may react, blame God and become bitter—thus revealing the flaws in our character. If our heart is right, we will trust God, confess His goodness, and humble ourselves under His hand—thus revealing our heart is right before the Lord. He then in turn blesses us for passing the test.

4. To prepare us for blessing.

"For the LORD your God is bringing you into a good land, a land of brooks of water, of fountains and springs, that flow out of valleys and hills; a land of wheat and barley, of vines and fig trees and pomegranates, a land of olive oil and honey; a land in which you will eat bread without scarcity, in which you will lack nothing; a land whose stones are iron and out of whose hills you can dig copper. When you have eaten and are full, then you shall bless the LORD your God for the good land which He has given you."
(Deuteronomy 8:7-10)

God wants you to be able to handle the blessing when it comes. Often God will allow famine to train us to be good managers during the lean times so that we will have the wisdom, discipline, and integrity to handle the good times of blessing.

A friend of mine had a woman in his church win the lottery. In an instant, she went from one income level to another that involved millions of dollars. The woman did not honor the Lord by tithing (giving ten percent), neither did she have the management or wisdom to handle the abundance. Within a few years, she went from multi-millionaire to poverty because she was not prepared for the abundance. Now I am not an advocate of the lottery, but this story illustrates how not being prepared for abundance sets you up for failure. God wants us to retain the abundance, blessing, and prosperity that He gives. In order to train us to handle the blessing, He sometimes allows famine to equip us.

How Do I Face Famine With Faith?

There is a simple science experiment that illustrates a powerful point. In the experiment we would take an empty 2-Liter bottle, and fill it up half way with water and the other half with vegetable oil. Then we shake that bottle up and mixing the oil and water together. What's going to happen?

Well, you can shake that bottle all day, but as soon as you stop shaking it, the oil and the water are going to separate from each other in a matter of seconds. Why? Because oil and water are "polar opposites" of each other. These two substances have a totally different chemical make-up from each other, which makes it impossible for them to mix together. Polar opposites just don't mix. That is the way faith and unbelief work.

You are going to live out this law of famine and faith. It is unavoidable. At some point in your life you will be tested with a famine. When that time comes, either you are going to live life in faith or you are going to try to keep all of your seed and not plant a thing, when really God wants you to sow in famine and just trust him. The problem is it doesn't make sense. To the natural mind it seems foolish to sow seed in famine. But when God has spoken to you, there must arise within you a spirit of faith that overcomes the doubt and pushes you to sow. It is the ultimate statement of trust when, at God's Word, you sow in a time of famine. Sowing in famine is not logical. It is not reasonable. Yet God's word does not say, "The just shall live by reason or logic." It boldly declares that "The just shall live by faith," (Romans

1:17; Hebrews 10:38) and also that we live "by every word the proceeds from the mouth of God." (Matthew 4:4)

You cannot expect to be blessed and be half faith and half unbelief. No matter how hard you try to shake and mix the two, you are still going to have unbelief in the mix and as long as you have unbelief or doubt you will not be able to handle your time of famine. You must be a person who stands in faith during famine!! The apostle James put it well when he said, "But let him ask in faith, *with no doubting*, for he who doubts is like a wave of the sea, driven and tossed by the wind. *Let not that man suppose he will receive anything from the Lord*." (James 1: 6-7 NKJV *emphasis mine*)

How To Face Your Famine With Faith

1. Listen to God's Word!

Every believer must do this. In this information age we have all kinds of sources for news. We hear this report and that report. We surf from one channel of bad news to another. What does *God* say to you?

This was the case in Genesis 26. Isaac was told, "Don't go to Egypt. Sow your seed." And he did. He listened to God's word. As he followed it, there was an amazing miracle!

Elsewhere in Scripture we see the prophet going to a widow. He boldly and audaciously tells the widow to give him something to eat. She had completely run out of food because of a famine in the land and was preparing one last meal for herself and her son. The widow had a choice right at that moment. She could have said, "No, I think you better go to the house down the road. That woman is a much better cook than I am!!" But she didn't. She listened to the word of God. As a result the Lord blessed her with more than food in the midst of famine!!

We have the example of the disciples in Mark 6 of the hungry multitude and almost nothing to give them to eat. The disciples could have said, "I don't know what you are thinking Jesus, but we've got five loaves and two fish and we've got 5000 men, not counting women and children. How are we going to feed them with five loaves and two fish?" But they listened to Jesus' word. They listened to the word of God. In Jesus' words to feed the multitude was the source of faith to face their famine.

Remember, faith comes by hearing a word from God. This is why we must be taking in the scriptures on a daily basis! It is our source of faith! To face famine with faith you must listen to God's Word! It is His manual for every situation in life. And when we are faced with famine we must believe that if we sow seed and follow the word of God, we will find blessing. Even though everyone else around me is in famine, I'm going to be blessed.

2. Believe and confess that it is God's will to prosper you.

There was a time in my life when I wasn't sure about this. I believed God wanted to prosper and bless me, but my doctrine was based on earning God's blessing. As I have studied God's Word it has become very clear that God wants to bless me just because I am His child. He wants to bless you in the same way. We can't *earn* His favor. We just have it. It's because of His mercy and goodness. He is a good God and wants to bless us!

There is a powerful pattern of God's blessing, provision and prosperity through the history of His people. God miraculously delivered Israel from Egypt (the land of not enough). He then lead them through the wilderness (the land of just enough). And finally brought them into the Promised Land (the land of more than enough).

EGYPT	WILDERNESS	CANAAN
Bondage	Wandering	Promised Land
Land of Not enough	*Land of Just Enough*	*Land of More Than Enough*
God Provided: Food during slavery; Silver, Gold & Clothing during the Exodus	God Provided: Water & Manna; Cloud & Fire; Quail; 40 year sandals	God Provided: Milk & Honey; Silver & Gold; Brass & Iron; Houses & Lands; Cities & Vineyards; Success & Victory

I took this to heart and began allowing it to influence how I prayed. I began driving through my community and praying over vacant lots and fields and declaring the blessing of God over them. I began to call in businesses and industry. I took authority over any spirit of poverty that would have a foothold and I boldly declared the blessing, favor, and prosperity of God. Over the next few years those vacant lots and fields were developed and major businesses and stores moved in! At the time there were no Starbucks stores in our community, but over the course of the next few years four Starbucks stores opened and now I am in coffee heaven!!

Some people would just credit this to coincidence or the natural development of a growing community. Not me. I prayed and it happened. God answered my prayers and blessed my community. Friend, your prayers work. God delights in answering them! If you will stand in faith, even when confronted with famine, He will answer you and bless you! Begin praying for blessing in your community. Start declaring God's Word over the empty, broken, and famine-stricken areas of your city or community and watch as God moves! It may take a few months or even years, but God will respond and He will bless. He wants to build His kingdom there! He wants to establish His covenant with people in your city! Deuteronomy 8:18 says, "And you shall remember the Lord your God, for it is He that gives you the power to get wealth, that He may establish His covenant…" If you are blessed, then you have more to give. As you give more, the kingdom of God has more. And as a result, those resources work to establish God's covenant in your community!

3. Forsake any poverty mindset that has influence in your life.

I'll give you an example of a poverty mindset. Someone once told me, "I can't afford to tithe." That is a poverty mindset. When they bought into that way of thinking, they sentenced themselves to live under poverty. As a believer, God is to have the pre-eminence in our lives. He must be first. When we give we must follow the pattern for giving in the scriptures. God's economy is based on giving. The starting point—let me say it again—the starting point for every believer is the tithe or ten percent (The word "tithe" literally means *a tenth*). Unfortunately, too many Christians are living in poverty because they believe that they can't afford to tithe. God took into account every conceivable financial situation and still instituted the tithe. He is not shocked about the place you are in. The Lord is not surprised by your economic plight. He has known about it all along. The key to getting out of poverty and into blessing is changing poverty thinking patterns and replacing them with thoughts of faith.

Poverty thinking is not faith thinking. It is rooted in pity, negativity, jealousy, envy, and doubt. In order to loosen the chains of lack off of your life, you must accept by faith what the Scriptures tell us about God's economic plan. Once you believe the biblical doctrine of prosperity for a purpose, you must practice its principles. A good work ethic, sound money management, and a generous giving commitment are all solid foundations for building a life of blessing— even during famine! The key starting point is your mindset.

4. Realize that famine is a test.

We read Deuteronomy 8 and we know this is true. I believe this was also a test in Elijah's life (1 Kings 17). He prophesied that a famine would come and when it arrived, it affected his life personally. Wouldn't it be nice if God somehow protected his faithful prophet from the famine? But instead, that which he prophesied affected his life as well. But even in the midst of the famine, God provided for his servant. When famine comes into your life it tests you in several ways.

- A test of your heart.

This is where God wants to know if you are handling money or if money is handling you. It is also the acid test of your love for God. The Bible says, "Where your treasure is there your heart will be also." (Matthew 6:21) Famine comes and tests your treasure. And if it affects your treasure to the point where it hurts your faith in God, you've got a little too much faith in the treasure and you need to stretch your faith in God. Your faith must not be in the treasure. Your faith must be in God.

Pastoring in a community with a heavy military influence can have its challenges. At one point, the base in our community was on the pentagon's base closure list. Rumor had it that it was very likely that our base would close. It would have immense financial repercussions for our region. I was in prayer one day asking for God's help regarding this situation. I was very concerned and the Lord spoke these words, "Who is your source? The military base? Is it the government?" In that moment I knew that I was relying on the treasure and not on my Provider. And so I just began to say, "Yes that is true. Lord, I believe you. I believe that whether this military base comes or goes, You are going to bless this community. My faith is in You. There are people to be saved here and You have a church that needs to fulfill the Commission. There is a covenant that needs to be established here and I know that in order for us to do these things, it takes resources to do them. I know that in order to have resources, there is going to have to be some kind of provision that is going to promote and bring in those kinds of resources into our community. So Lord, I trust You, because You are my Source!" I prayed that prayer and placed my faith where it should have been—in the Lord. He used that situation to test my heart.

- A test of your motives.

This test has to do with the "why" of our giving and generosity. When you give to the Lord, you give to people. I remember when Cheryl and I were first married there was a time in our lives when we bought a bunch of groceries for some people and left them at their doorstep. It was during a period in our life when we weren't making very much money. It was tight. It was lean. And the Lord directed us to go and give all those groceries away to somebody else. We could have used that food, but that wasn't the point. God was teaching us to love Him by loving people. He was teaching us to give without expecting anything in return. Just do it to be a blessing. It was His way of testing our motives.

Often there is a hook in our giving. We put it out there so that it will come back. Now clearly the bible teaches the principle of sowing and reaping. It is an undeniable truth. Yet it must not be our driving motive. Our motives are tested in famine. God will make sure that our giving is centered around love. We must not give to get something back. Your motive must always be to show love, the love of the Lord—that you love God and that you love people.

• A test of your obedience.

It's easy to obey God when everything is good. The grass is green. Life is good. The bank account is full. You have some money to save. You have some money to invest. You are driving that new car. You are closing that new house. Hallelujah! You want me to give? No problem! Doing a building fund at the church? Yeah! Write that check. When things are good it is really easy to do that. What happens when famine strikes? "Well I don't know if I am going to be able to make my house payment. I have no money going into savings. I have no money going into retirement. I haven't had a sale in God knows when." And you're waiting, and waiting, and waiting. It's easy to obey when money is good. It's not so easy when it is hard. When it's "famine hard."

During famine is when you've got to make a decision based on principle. Now you've got to make a decision based on obedience. Cheryl and I decided to raise our giving—to go beyond our normal tithe and other giving. Once we did it, there were times when it was tight. There were weeks when it was very hard to give that extra amount. But we believed that we had heard from the Lord and we buckled down and followed through out of obedience. Now my obedience is not based on some legalistic bondage, but on a true love for God and His kingdom. Our obedience is driven by love and enacted out of conviction. Obedience is rarely convenient or comfortable. Famine is allowed by God to test our obedience. In testing our obedience God is also testing our convictions and our love for Him.

And you know what? We've seen God come through time and again. During this time there was a month when we weren't sure if we were going to make our house payment. We'd spent some money elsewhere and we thought we were going to have money for our house payment. We didn't know what we were going to do, but we kept faithful in our new giving commitment. At one point my wife said, "Well maybe I'll call my dad and ask him for the money, the extra money to help push us over so we can make our house payment." At that moment, the Heavenly Father spoke to her and said, "Why don't you just ask me? I'm your Dad. I've got all the money in the world." And she replied, "Ok. Heavenly Father, we need money for our house payment." Within in a few days we got four times our house payment, unsolicited, unasked for, totally out of the blue! We got a gift four times the amount of our house payment. Why is that? Why does that happen? Because you obey God and He is good. I believe it happened because we were obeying the Lord. We were fulfilling our commitment to Him.

• A test of your humility.

God will use famine to test your humility. Remember in Deuteronomy why He tests us? To humble you. He says that three times. God wants us to rely on Him and not on our own strength. We can humble ourselves or be humbled. I choose to humble myself. Because the "be humbled" thing is not fun. We need to let the Lord speak to us and then humble ourselves right away. Too often people allow money, status, or possessions to define them. Others will make these things trophies of their accomplishments— all designed to build themselves up. Having this attitude is an affront to God. It is proud and arrogant—both things which God hates. God will allow famine into our lives to keep our spirit free from pride and arrogance. It is part of His process for working humility into our lives.

There's a story of a man who had a high opinion of himself and he stepped on a coin-operated scale that dispensed a card, giving his weight and comments about his personality. After reading the card, he handed it to his wife and said, "Here, look at this!" She took it and read aloud, "You are dynamic, a born leader, handsome, and much admired by women for your personality." Giving it a second look, she added, "Hmmm, I see it's got your weight wrong too!" Humble yourself and it won't be so bad if you are humbled.

* A test of your confidence.

Where do we put our confidence? You don't live by the money you make, but by the provision of the Lord! What does the book of Acts say? "In Him we live, move and have our being." (Acts 17:28) All the things that you need in this tight time are in Him. The house payment that we need to make is in Him. That car payment is in Him. Your favorable job interview is in Him. Yes, there are things that you must do. I'm not saying you sit on your hands expecting God to just give you a job. The point is that our confidence must be in Him.

5. Give your way out of famine.

One of the most incredibly impoverished places I have ever been in the world is India. From the moment you enter their culture you are confronted with abject poverty. It was to this culture that Teresa came to bring God's love and Good News. She left a life of wealth and status to go to India. All of the comforts and niceties of her home and family were given up to accomplish her mission. Most of us know her by her title name – Mother Teresa. She once said, "If you give what you do not need, it isn't giving." Not only did she believe this, Mother Teresa lived this truth out in her everyday life for decades. When she died, she had raised millions of dollars and had started orphanages and aid organizations all over the world and in the nation of India. She was an amazing person who understood that breaking the back of famine starts with a giving heart and life.

For every Christian our starting point is that 10% of giving that is known as the *tithe*. For some of you, starting there is a sacrifice in any economy, but when it is a season of famine, it is even more difficult. You may be one of those who say, "But I need that 10%." Yeah, you probably do. But you need to give it anyway. What you are doing is participating in the Divine Economy. God has a Divine Economy and it doesn't work by the world's standards. The world says, "Get and you will have something to give." The Bible says, "Give and you will get something back out of it." The world says, "Well I need to receive some seed so that I can sow to reap." The Bible says, "No, just sow and you will reap." You will reap seed back. You will reap bread back. The law of the kingdom is totally different than the law of the world. We need to give our way out of famine.

I've proven this over and over in my life. And if you read the life story of Mother Teresa you know that was exactly how she lived her life. Giving her way through life. In one of her journals she wrote how she has never, ever lacked for a meal in her entire ministry. Not one time. She chose to fast at certain times. But she never lacked. And God brought supply into her life in incredible ways. The sisterhood that she established brought in millions of dollars over her lifetime into meeting the needs in Calcutta. Why did that happen? Because she just gave. Even though she lived in famine. She just gave and gave and gave and gave. She stared down famine with eyes of compassion and a giving heart. Mother Teresa overcame famine with faith and giving.

6. Manage your resources wisely.

Gen. 41 we hear the story of how Joseph handled the famine with faith and stewardship (7 yrs. of plenty & 7 yrs. of famine). Joseph deals with the famine by good stewardship. There's a lot that can be said about faith, there's a lot of that can be said about prosperity. But there is a lot that needs to be said about paying your bills, making your payments on time, having good credit, being a good steward of what God has given you. One of the ways to face famine with faith is to be a good steward over what you do have.

There was that old lady in the New Testament that gave those two mites. She gave all that she had to the Lord because evidently that was the best stewardship of what she had, was to give it to the Lord. Some people are in that place where what they have in their hand (or bank account) will not meet their need. It may be that if it does not meet your need—it may be your seed.

I know of a man who was in a church meeting and the Holy Spirit spoke to him to give to a certain cause in the church. As he waited for the divine direction, God spoke clearly into his heart, "I want you to write a check for all that is in your account—give it all!" Now I don't recommend this to you. This isn't a word of advice to anybody. I'm just telling you the story. Stunned, the man sat in his seat evaluating this massive decision. Personally, he needed the money. But, out of faith and obedience he wrote the check and gave it. The next week a man came to him and offered to buy his business for this insane amount of money. But here's the kicker—he could then buy back the business for one dollar and continue to run the company and pay this investor a percentage of the profits. Out of that one act of obedience and faith, this man now had the resources to do what was his dream—live on about 40% of his income and the other 60% he gives away to the poor and to the kingdom of God. But it all came down to the decision to obey the voice of the Lord and do what He told him to do. "I want you to give everything."

Many people today have no concept of wise management of their resources. When they think of money, they think in terms of where they are going to spend it. Let me ask you, do you balance your checkbook regularly? Do you have a monthly budget? Are you living within your means? If you answer "No" to any of these questions, you need to change. You are not handling your resources wisely. The harsh reality is that when you face times of famine, instead of overcoming them, they will eat your lunch and pop the sack too! There are many excellent tools and helps that can be beneficial for you. Dave Ramsey's *Financial Peace University* is a wonderful resource. It will equip you with tools you need to manage your resources with wisdom.

Moving through famine takes more than faith—it takes wisdom too. Wisdom is the sister to faith. She keeps faith balanced and in check. Wisdom helps us to guard against living foolishly in the name of faith.

These six things will work in your life to bring you through times of famine. They have worked in my life. They will work in your life. They are straight from the Bible. These principles are how faith, when it really matters most, can come into your life and change it for good and help you break out of famine and into feasting!

Chapter 9
Standing Fast In Faith

"Watch, stand fast in the faith, be brave, be strong."
1 Corinthians 16:13 NKJV

One Sunday morning before church someone asked me how my week was. Without giving too many details, I replied, "Interesting." They gave me a quizzical look and waited for particulars. I was not about to delve into it with them. The week had been one of "those" weeks. Have you ever had one of "those" weeks? I had planned projects and meetings. There was a course of action set and ready to go—and not one thing happened according to the plan. I was frustrated, irritated, and disappointed in what I thought was an unproductive week.

My wife is a woman with a plan. She thinks details and plans. There are lists and goals. She is truly an amazing woman!! She runs our home very well and is a phenomenal mom to our kids. If there is a vacation coming up, she wants to know the plan. If there is a holiday or birthday, "What's the plan?" We discuss the plan. We write the plan. We budget the plan. We plan plans within the plan to accomplish the plan!! When things do not go according to the plan—let's just say, it's not good.

During a time when things were not going according to her plan, Cheryl was praying and poured out her frustration to the Lord. "Things are not going according to plan! It's frustrating and I feel so out of control! If there was only a formula—some wondrous recipe for plan success! Why can't you give me something where I just do it and every time it works?!" The Lord gently responded to her, "Well, Cheryl, if I gave you a magic formula that worked every time, then you would trust in the formula instead of trusting in Me." Now that is the heart of the matter. Trust. It's not really about the plan. It's not really about the project. Most of the time when things don't go according to plan it is about—trust.

You may have read this book to this point and still remain doubtful or even skeptical of God's plan and purpose for you. Somewhere in a corner of your heart you think, "This is just not for me. I have had too many bad things happen—too many negative experiences. I understand what you are saying, Marc, but I just don't think this is for me." Friend, if there is even a flicker of faith in your heart, please activate it now and stand on it. No matter how small, weak, or even damaged your faith may be right now, hear the call of God to you to "Stand fast in that faith!"

The Call to Stand Fast

1 Corinthians 16:13 "Watch, *stand fast* in the faith, be brave, be strong." (emphasis mine)

This scripture is right at the end of Paul's first letter to the Corinthians. God is speaking to the church in Corinth. Paul founded this church and was speaking to them as a spiritual father. He has already addressed so many issues—disunity, divisive behavior, sin and compromise, spiritual gifts, and many other things. Now he is closing with possibly his most important commands and directions to them. And his final words were to "watch" (be alert and vigilant), "stand fast in the faith" (be immovable in your faith), "be brave" (stand with courage), and "be strong" (full of strength and endurance). These were not the flippant words of a novice, but they were the solemn charge of the apostle in his closing remarks to the Corinthian church. It's almost as if he is saying, "If you get nothing else, get this!" Standing fast in faith is second in his top four things! In Paul's mind this was very important!

Gary Smalley tells the story of a time when he was deep in the woods hunting with a friend. All of a sudden a deep pain struck him in the chest and he collapsed to the ground — he knew immediately he was having a massive heart attack. When he got to the hospital, one of his sons came to him and Gary began telling his son how much he loved him, and how much he cared for him, because he knew that his life was slipping away and any second he was going to be leaving his family and be right in the presence of the Lord. He looked into the eyes of his son and tried to verbalize all of those things he wanted to say in those last few moments. It was the moment of life and death. In that moment, you aren't going to say, "Hey, don't forget to brush your teeth tonight before you go to bed." Those are not the things you talk about. You talk about the things that mean the most to you in that moment. His son looked into his eyes and said, "I know Dad. I know." It's a very important thing to look at this scripture and recognize that these are the apostle's last words to them in this epistle. Paul is saying the most important things he can say. And he's saying, "Watch, stand fast in the faith, be brave, be strong."

2 Corinthians 1:24 declares, "Not that we have dominion over your faith, but are fellow workers for your joy; for *by faith you stand.*" (emphasis mine)

THE MESSAGE – "…you stand by your own faith, not by ours."

You are going to stop reading this book and you are going to face all of the things your future holds – the challenges, famine, fear, attacks to your health. The list is endless. You are not going to face them on *my* faith. You are going to face them on *your faith*. What you've got. And the question is, "At the end of the day, when you close this book, are you going to have the faith to face those things or not?" You cannot rise on the coattails of your parent's faith, or your girlfriend's faith, or even the faith of your pastor. The faith that gets you through all of life's challenges and struggles is *your faith!* This is the faith that matters most.

So let me ask you, how's your faith? Is it weak? Strong? Do you have merely a religious and traditional faith system or is your faith living, dynamic, personal, and life-giving? What condition is your faith in? It is a very important question because you can only stand in your own faith. Your faith is the faith that matters most.

Ephesians 6:13-14a "Therefore take up the whole armor of God, that you may be able to *withstand* in the evil day, and having done all, to *stand*. *Stand* therefore..." (emphasis mine)

In these few scriptural phrases the word "stand" is used three times. When you are in the fight of faith, when you need to resist the devil, when the enemy is coming against you like a flood, you need to stand fast in the faith. Do not be swayed. Do not be overwhelmed. (cf. 1 Peter 5:9) Do not give in to the temptation to give up—even when you feel you have tried everything and nothing seems to work. The bible is very clear here, "...and having done all, to stand..." This means when you have tried every option and you have examined every route, and nothing is working—stand fast. Don't quit. Don't give up. Don't surrender ground. Stand fast.

You can almost hear the expectation in the apostle's command. "Stand, because God is working. Things are going to change. The wall is going to break. There is a shift coming. Just stand and watch the hand of God work." That expectation is the faith part of standing fast. It is faith that empowers the person to stand. Faith sees the invisible, but inevitable victory. Faith sees the coming breakthrough. Because of this faith you are able to stand fast.

Philippians 1:27 "Only let your conduct be worthy of the gospel of Christ, so that whether I come and see you or am absent, I may hear of your affairs, *that you stand fast* in one spirit, with one mind striving together for the faith of the gospel" (emphasis mine)

Paul uses strong terms here as he calls us to stand fast. He uses the phrase, "let your conduct be worthy of the gospel of Christ..." The term "worthy" is from the Greek word *axios* which is a word that describes value based on weight. In Paul's time, gold or silver was weighed on scales and, according to the weight of the gold or silver in the coin, a value was given. That assigned value determined what the coin was worth.

When Paul tells us that our conduct must be worthy of the gospel of Christ, he is reminding us that our life of faith must have weight and substance to it. It cannot be some light commitment to Christ and His purpose for our lives, but the life we live must be "heavy" and full of substance. His first criteria for having a life worthy of the gospel is that we "stand fast." Our faith cannot be a 'light-weight' faith, but a faith with significant value. Our life of faith must be weighty and not easily swayed by our feelings, circumstances, or troubles. Your ability to stand fast in faith makes your faith all the more valuable.

Colossians 1:21-23 "And you, who once were alienated and enemies in your mind by wicked works, yet now He has reconciled in the body of His flesh through death, to present you holy, and blameless, and above reproach in His sight—if indeed you *continue in the faith, grounded and steadfast, and are not moved* away from the hope of the gospel which you heard, which was preached to every creature under heaven, of which I, Paul, became a minister." (emphasis mine)

"Continue in the faith." It sounds simple. But these four words are not a description of some simple religious exercise. Continuing in faith is the result of total abandoned commitment to one's faith. Today we enjoy incredible access to music through digital means. CD's, mp3 players, and other devices stream symphonic delight into our cars, homes, computers, and even our workouts. We probably would not have these amazing technologies if it weren't for the phonograph. The phonograph was a device that recorded sounds. It's inventor, Thomas Edison was an incredible genius who knew what it meant to continue until a project was done. "Work," he said, "is measured not by hours, but by what it accomplished." He even had a clock without hands on his desk. Edison believed that rewarding work called for 2% inspiration and 98% perspiration. Continuing in faith is a lot like that.

I have known many people who start things, but never finish them. They start out fast and full of excitement, but after a few disappointments or delays to their plans, they quit. Friend, you cannot take that approach to faith. You must continue in it. In order to do this, we must be "grounded and steadfast, and...not moved." Standing fast in your faith is the key to enduring faith. You are not called to live a flippant faith, but an enduring faith!! The writer to the book of Hebrews tells us that we must "run with endurance the race that is set before us." (Hebrews 12:1 NKJV) Jesus said that we must have a faith that will endure the storms of life and not fall. (Matthew 7:24-27) This is not shallow faith. It is not emotional faith. You cannot live enduring faith as long as it is based on life's circumstances. No, we are called to finish our race with joy, strength, and determination. Be grounded and steadfast, in other words immovable. Don't be moved. Don't be swayed. Don't be overwhelmed. Don't be shaken. Don't be doubtful. Don't be intimidated by the enemy. Don't be overcome in your faith. Stand, steadfast in faith!

We must be people of faith who know how to "stand fast – to not quit, give up, or move. These are times when it would be easy to run from the situation, but instead we must determine to hang in there and not move—to stand fast. The faith that matters most is the kind that stands fast! This kind of faith is not easy. Too often people waver in their faith, and wavering faith is not without great risks.

The Risks of Wavering Faith

Abraham is our father in faith. (Galatians 3:7, 9) Even though his faith was tested, Scripture tells us that he did not waver in his faith (Romans 4:20). Even though God's promise to Abraham was impossible, the patriarch believed God with unreserved confidence. He trusted God with his whole heart and overcame everything that may have impeded his trust. One may even translate Romans 4:20 to say, "He was not inwardly divided…" Often we become "inwardly divided" by doubting God's promise or questioning His word to us. I know people who move between "maybe He will" to "maybe He won't" – as if they are plucking the petals from a flower playing 'He loves me—He loves me not.' The apostle James tells us that if we waver in this way, we shouldn't expect to receive anything from the Lord. (James 1:7) Wow! What a risk we take when we waver in our faith! The risks of wavering faith are on many levels and have consequences when we give in to them.

1. When we waver in faith, we risk our example.

One of my life verses is 1 Timothy 4:12. As a teenager, I latched on to this verse and made it a part of my spirit. I knew if I pursued what this passage declared, I would not only fulfill God's purpose for my life, but I would do it in power! Paul is mentoring his protégé, Timothy, who was a young man and a leader of one of the most influential churches in the New Testament. The apostle tells his spiritual son, "Let no one despise your youth, but be an example to believers." Timothy is given a checklist of things that he should be an example in. One of those important exemplary traits is faith.

Every person is to be a model of steadfast faith. Not just preachers. Not just pastors. Every one of us are supposed to be able to say, "Follow me as I follow Christ." And if we are going to say that, then we need to demonstrate follow-able faith. You must have faith that is worthy to be followed.

If the example we provide is one of weak faith, we will produce weak disciples with even weaker faith than our own. A powerful law of discipleship is: those who follow often do in excess what you do in moderation. So, if we are wavering in our faith, those to whom we are an example (our children, co-workers, neighbors, friends, etc.) most likely will waver even more in their faith. If you waiver in doubt and unbelief, and you question the promises of God and the future that God has for your life, or you doubt whether God is really with you, the people who are following you are going to be even greater doubters than you. When we waver in faith, we risk our example.

2. When we waver in faith, we risk departing from the faith, being deceived, and entering into foolishness.

1 Timothy 4:1-3 "Now the Spirit expressly says that in latter times some will depart from the faith, giving heed to deceiving spirits and doctrines of demons, speaking lies in hypocrisy, having their own conscience seared with a hot iron, forbidding to marry, and commanding to abstain from foods which God created to be received with thanksgiving by those who believe and know the truth." (NKJV)

When we do not stay steadfast in our faith, we risk moving from wavering faith to abandoned faith. I can't think of anything more tragic than for someone to abandon their faith. I have seen it happen. Some young man or woman enters into trying times, and instead of investing in their faith and burrowing deeper into faith, they become weaker and waver more and more. Eventually, with wavering and weak faith going unchecked, they abandon their faith altogether.

The Bible teaches us that, "just as you have received Christ, so you must continue to follow Him." (Colossians 2:6 NLT) Our journey with Christ started in faith. We must continue in our journey in a strong spirit of faith. If your faith is not steadfast, you will eventually lose your moorings in "the faith." If you are "Joe Vacillation" or "Mary Rollercoaster" in your faith—up and down and everywhere—then that instability of faith places you at risk. Some people's faith is like watching a pinball machine, bouncing from crisis to crisis, not knowing what's going to happen next. That is not biblical faith. Biblical faith is proactive. It is acting on God's Word and initiating positive actions and plans to fulfill God's purpose. Too often people live pinball faith—reactionary faith—simply reacting to life's challenges, often in a negative way, with no clue as to what God's purpose is or how to fulfill it. Just as a pinball machine has a "tilt" mechanism in it when the game is bumped too wildly, so people will "tilt" and everything shuts down. They have wavered so much that they completely withdraw their faith, abandoning their hope in God and their conviction that His purpose for their lives will be fulfilled. I have seen this acted out in so many people. Right at the point when faith matters most and it's time to dig in, they throw up their hands in despair and quit.

Now your life may feel like a pinball machine, but faith says, "I don't really understand what is happening, but my eyes are on the Lord. And I know that faithful is He who called me, Who will also do what I've committed to His trust. He that began a good work in me I know will complete it!" It probably sounds strange to hear yourself confess this, but I urge you right now to pause and declare those previous words. They are faith statements about your future and your life. Even though you may feel like that steel ball bouncing all around that pinball machine, you are able to say in a spirit of faith, "I don't know how it is all going to end up, but I know that God is able to make it all turn out for good." How does that happen? Where does a statement like that come from? Steadfastness of faith.

I have to say a word about deception here. Once a person becomes frustrated with the perceived failure of faith, they will open the door to deceiving spirits and doctrines of demons. This is prophesied by the Holy Spirit in 1 Timothy 4:1-3. In the Old Testament, King Saul is a prime example of this principle. Once a man who was committed to following God, he later began to waver in faith. Out of impatience and frustration, he begins resisting God and wavering even more in faith. Finally, after abandoning his trust in God, he actually consults with a witch and the next day dies in battle. Often people become embittered because of disappointed faith. That bitterness acts like a poison to the soul and eventually their poisoned heart becomes distorted and darkened—opening up doors of access to demonic spirits who will torment and deceive them.

Is your faith frustrated? Have you questioned God's goodness and His motives of love for you because of the contradictions to His promise? My friend, I urge you with all my heart to not allow that frustration to turn to angry bitterness. Do not become offended at God. Instead, go back to His Word and remind yourself of how good He is. Remember that He loves you and will never leave you or forsake you. Slam the door on those whispering voices that are trying to convince you that God doesn't care. He does care. He is a good God and He will turn it all around for good!

3. When we waver in faith, we risk condemnation and losing our bearings in life.

1 Timothy 5:12 talks about those who struggle with "having condemnation because they have cast off their first faith." There are many Christians who have experienced some problem, or delay, or famine, or some other test of their faith, and have assumed it is God rejecting them. They believe there has been some great sin or evil in their life and they come under condemnation. They often ask, "What did I do to deserve this?" Or they turn it on God with some question like, "Well, if God is so good, why did this horrible thing happen to me?" Believe me, I've been there. I have been tempted to go there many times. But somewhere in my heart, I know that those thoughts and feelings do not line up with God's

Word. Now, don't get me wrong—I pray some pretty harsh prayers to God at times. They are what I like to call "honest-to-God" prayers. But somewhere along the line, there must be an acknowledgement that we have weaknesses and God is working on those to make us stronger. We must resist the temptation to receive condemnation, and instead stir our faith to face our weaknesses and change them with the power of the Holy Spirit!

Because of the condemnation, doubt, and questions that fill people's minds, they lose their confidence and direction. Pretty soon they are just drifting around doing nothing—and feeling guilty about it! And they have this condemnation and false guilt. They assume that, because the plan is not working, there is something wrong with them. With some of the challenges we have faced together, my wife would be free to admit that there have been times in her life when the plan was not working and she would ask God, "What's wrong with me?" And God would reply, "There's nothing wrong with you! This is just part of the process and journey of faith." She responds and renews her mind and changes her focus. But so many of us get caught up with "What's wrong with me? I just don't know what is wrong with me!" And that is the breeding ground for doubt and mistrust of God. What's soon to follow is the loss of purpose and then your life becomes a meandering path—without purpose and meaning.

I have noticed that when some people get to this point, instead of taking responsibility for their wavering faith, they often try to compensate by blaming other people. "Well, if Pastor So and So was a better mentor, then things would have turned out a lot better." Or, "If my boss wasn't such a jerk, then I would have been more successful here!" As you can see, this blame game often takes the form of gossip and other destructive behaviors. If you are reading this and seeing yourself here, please take a moment right now to ask God to stabilize your faith. Ask Him for the grace to take responsibility for where you are and ask Him to forgive you if you have participated in any gossip or destructive behaviors that are often found in the "blame game."

4. When we waver in faith, we risk falling prey to greed and its sorrows.

1 Timothy 6:10 *"For the love of money is a root of all kinds of evil, for which **some have strayed from the faith** in their greediness, and pierced themselves through with many sorrows."*(Emphasis mine) How a person views money and possessions is a powerful acid test for their faith. This scripture was not written only for the rich, but for everyone. Over the years I have become friends with some very wealthy people. They are sweet, godly people who give generously and it is very clear that what drives them is their faith, not their finances. On the other hand, I have known poor folks as well. And interestingly, they often seem bitter and stingy—even greedy. In fact, it may surprise you to know that some of the most of the greedy people I have known are those without much money or possessions.

What does this have to do with my faith? Faith will demonstrate its strength through wise money management and generous giving. How a person handles their money and possessions is a clue to their strength of faith. A person's attitude towards money and possessions is another indicator to their strength of faith. If you grumble when you give, it is likely that money has gotten a hold of your heart. When you give, you feel like you are losing something. A person of faith believes that when they give they are investing in something. It is a completely different perspective.

The man Job is a powerful example of this. The devil, wanting to destroy Job's faith, asked God if he could take his wealth and possessions. The devil was sure that Job would blame God, get bitter, and desert his faith. God knew Job's heart. He knew Job had the right spirit of faith towards his wealth. And when the devil destroyed Job's' wealth—Job remained strong in faith. Job boldly declared, "Though God kill me, yet I will trust Him!" His strong, unwavering faith, guarded him from greed. And when his wealth disappeared, his faith stood strong.

This is why it is so important to give our tithe and offerings to God. It is an act of faith. Every time you give you are saying that your faith is not in your money, but in God. Your faith is not in the provision, but in the Provider.

5. When we waver in faith, we risk our righteousness.

Philippians. 3:9 speaks of the "righteousness which is from God by faith." Elsewhere the Bible tells us that, "Abraham believed God and it was accounted to him for righteousness." (Romans 4:3). When we become doubters, tolerating a spirit of unbelief or an attitude of negativity, it will eventually affect your righteousness. It will affect your ability to stand right before God. Things will not be right, they will be wrong.

Romans. 14:23 declares, "...for whatever is not from faith is sin." What is the opposite of faith? Unbelief. Again and again God disciplined His people because of this sin. To not believe is to violate the very essence of being a Christian. We are BELIEVERS! Everything we receive from God is "by grace through faith." We are made righteous by believing in Christ's work on the cross. To not believe doesn't change the power of His sacrifice, but it does neutralize its affect on the sin in our lives. For Jesus' sacrifice to become effective in us, we must believe in it by faith. The righteousness of a person's life depends on that person's willingness to believe—have faith in—Jesus Christ. To not believe is to choose to remain bound and dead in your unrighteousness and sin. Let me say it plainly — to not respond in a spirit of faith is sin! So if you are habitually slipping into doubt, and wavering in your faith, then you are drifting in your faith. And like a wave of the sea, driven and tossed by the wind, you will be driven by life's circumstances, personal weaknesses, and deceptive spirits, into a "shipwrecked" state. There, with your faith gone and broken, you will go back to a life of sin and will become bound again to unrighteousness. People who end up like this are in active rebellion against the word of faith, which is sin and unbelief, and it will affect their righteousness.

I have seen this lived out in people's lives again and again. I urge you to evaluate your faith and if it is weak or if you are intensely struggling with doubt, let this be a wake-up call to you to strengthen your faith and by doing so strengthen yourself to walk in "the righteousness which is from God by faith."

6. We risk shipwreck if we do not stand fast in the faith.

I've never been in a shipwreck, but I have had to spend the night on an island in the San Juan Islands because my boat didn't work. Just that alone was bad enough.

1 Timothy 1:18-19 "This charge I commit to you, son Timothy, according to the prophecies previously made concerning you, that by them you may wage the good warfare, *having faith* and a good conscience, which some having rejected, *concerning the faith have suffered shipwreck.*" (emphasis mine)

The apostle Paul is giving a charge to Timothy, an apostolic command, regarding prophecies that he has received over his life. Paul tells Timothy to do three key things. First, "wage a good warfare." Second, "have faith." And third, "keep a good conscience." Paul then warns Timothy that shipwreck awaits those who do fail "concerning the faith." Now, I believe that all three were important to the apostle, yet interestingly, he focuses on faith as the key.

One of my giftings is prophecy. I have been prophesying over people and in the church for years.

Having given prophetic words to literally thousands of people, I have noticed that the fulfillment of those words is primarily based on that person's spirit and attitude of faith towards the prophetic word. When a person receives a prophecy, God is speaking through a chosen vessel to the *potential* of a person. Some have taken prophecy as a guarantee of what God will do, and in taking this approach, sit back, relax, and do nothing about it. However, prophecy is given to a person to *activate* them. They must engage their faith if they are going to see the fulfillment of the prophetic word to them.

One of the great tragedies of the kingdom is when people with tremendous potential get "activated" by a prophetic word, and then after the initial excitement wears off, they become bitter towards God and the church for not "doing something." All the while, God is waiting for them to "do something" with the word that He gave them. These frustrated believers, often withdraw from the church, feed their disillusionment, and fall away from God. This is exactly what Paul was warning Timothy about—the risk of shipwreck when people do not stand fast in faith.

How Do I Stand Fast in Faith?

1. Be alert to your faith.

1 Corinthians 16:13 *"Watch, stand fast in the faith, be brave, be strong."*

"Watch" literally means *to give strict attention to, be cautious, active.* One bible dictionary defines it further: *To take heed lest through remission and indolence some destructive calamity suddenly overtake one.* In other words, pay attention as if your life or your faith depended on it. Because it does. Your future depends on it. Your faith depends on it.

2 Corinthians 13:5 *"Examine yourselves as to whether you are in the faith. Test yourselves. Do you not know yourselves, that Jesus Christ is in you? — unless indeed you are disqualified."*

Now he wouldn't talk about being disqualified if it wasn't possible. What should you do? Examine yourself. Know the state of your faith. Be alert to the condition of your heart. Pay attention to what's going on with your faith. Every day you need to get up and say, "I am not going to allow doubt or feelings of unbelief or questioning of God's love for me or any of those things to overwhelm my mind. I'm not even going to tolerate that kind of thinking." You must actively do this every day. If you don't, you are not being alert to your faith.

We can ask ourselves key questions to assess our faith. Am I struggling with doubt? Am I shifting into negativity without even realizing it? What has been my confession? Am I speaking things of faith or are they words of giving up, throwing in the towel, or despair. "Why bother?" or "This is totally going to fail!" are not words of faith. You are prophesying to your future before you even get started. Those aren't words of faith. Be alert to your faith.

2. Ground yourself in the Truth.

Romans 10:17 *"Faith comes by hearing...the word of God."*

John 17:17 *"Your Word is truth."*

I have come to realize that there is a difference between the facts and the truth.

The fact is your marriage can be on the rocks and it looks like it's about to fail. The Truth is God can restore anything.

The fact is it looks weak and bleak, but the Truth says, "in our weakness He is made strong!"

The fact is I can't do this, but the Truth says, "I can do all things through Christ Who strengthens me!"

The facts are I am alone and I feel alone, but the Truth is "He will never leave me or forsake me" and "I have a friend that sticks closer than a brother!"

The fact is I am at a stopping point, but the Truth is "I have put before you an open door that no man can shut!"

The fact is this is an impossible situation, but the Truth is "Nothing is impossible with God."

The fact is I am beaten, but the Truth is "I am more than a conqueror through Him Who loves me."

The fact is I am confused and hindered, but the Truth is "I will know the Truth and the Truth will make me free!"

There is a difference between the facts and the truth. And the Truth is always what you believe.

Philippians 4:8 says to meditate on these things—the first one? "Whatever things are **true!**"

A little thought pops into your mind, "Man does God even know I exist?" – is that true? What do you do with that thought? Cast it out. Confront it with the truth. Don't just say, "I don't believe that." Say, "I know and believe God cares for me!" Say it with your mouth. Confess it. A thought pops into your mind, "My Pastor doesn't care about my situation." That's not true. That is not the truth. Your pastor deeply cares for everybody in the church. He cares for the souls in your city. He prays for people all the time. He is deeply concerned with what is going on in your life. He may not be able to counsel every-body's every problem or pray for every single situation in life. Or walk with you to work, or walk with you to school or walk with you everywhere—he is not the Holy Spirit! But you can say, "I know my pastor loves me. I know he cares. I know he is for me and not against me." That is the truth. And so what do you think about? Think about whatsoever things are true.

3. Complain to God.

Did you just say complain? Absolutely. Complain to God. In Psalm 142 David pours out his complaint before God. When the Psalmist says, "I cry out to the Lord," he was probably crying and weeping. It may have even been laced with whining. Even the way David says his complaint is pretty bold. Go ahead. Be bold with God. He can handle it. He has handled running the universe with all its problems before you ever arrived. Do you think He is going to be taken unawares? "You complained!" God is not so insecure that if you complain to him He would worry about you attacking His integrity. God's not insecure. He can handle it.

Elsewhere the Bible says to "cast all your cares on Him for He cares for you." When you complain to God, go ahead and give yourself five minutes and just complain like crazy. Five minutes is a long time. Tell him how you feel. Tell him what you want. This is *Honest-To-God-Prayer*! "Man things are just terrible right now! I'm in a pit and things are just stinking—they are terrible! I'm lonely. I'm overwhelmed. I haven't had a good day in weeks! I don't know. It just feels like ..." Just go ahead. Five minutes.

Once your 5 minutes are up – fill your mouth with the positive confession of faith. Overcome those facts with the truth. Do it for ten minutes. Pray in faith and declare the goodness of God. Psalm 42 is our pattern. That is what David did. He started by pouring out his complaint to God, then, he ended with giving God a faithful declaration and interceding for his situation, and he did it in faith. Standing steadfast in faith.

DO NOT STAY IN THE COMPLAIN ZONE!! You should give at least twice as much time to faith as you do to complaining. Five minutes in the complain zone means ten minutes in the faith zone!

4. Lift up your eyes.

Heb. 12:2 "looking unto Jesus, the Author and the Finisher, of our faith…"

In the film, War of the Worlds, Tom Cruise plays a father who is trying to get his son and daughter to safety while the world is being attacked. At one point in the movie his character and daughter are in a horrible situation. In order to keep her sense of security and safety he tells her, "Look at me. I want you to look at me. Are you looking at me?" and he's carrying her and walking. "Are you looking at me? Look at my eyes. Look at my face. Don't look around you." They are walking through this terrible scene of devastation. But she keeps her eyes on him until they got into the vehicle and drove away. That is exactly what we need to do with Jesus. When you are in your time of trial, stop focusing on your problem. Your problem is not the problem. If you think you will find your solution by looking at the problem, you are wrong. You will find your solution by looking at the solution, not at the problem. And who is the Solution? God. Jesus. He knows the truth. He's got all the wisdom. He's got all the knowledge. He's got all the understanding. He knows exactly what you need. Jesus is saying, "Look at me. Keep your eyes on me. Look at me. Stop looking at the storm." When Peter was walking on the water, one of the greatest testimonies of faith in the Bible, the reason why he sank into the water is because he took his eyes off Jesus and looked at the storm. What was the first thing Jesus said to him, when he stretched out His hand? He said, "Look at Me. No Peter, get your eyes off the storm. Look at Me."

When I was teaching one of my kids to swim, we were in a pool while on vacation. He made some good progress in the local pool. But this one time I told him, "I want you to swim to me." And he's looking at me and standing at the edge of the pool. I would tell him, "Don't look at the water, look at me. Now, swim to me." So I'm standing in the deep part of the water and he's looking at me. He starts bending his legs, pumping up and down. He thinks he is going to jump to me. So I said, "Come on! Jump in the water and swim! Don't think about drowning. Don't think about dying. Don't think about anything. Look at me and swim!" Suddenly, he jumped off the edge, and Splash! He goes under and back on top of the water—panting. I squatted in the water and said, "Come on! You can do it! You are doing great! Come on you can do it! No, don't look at the water. Look at me. Right here! Look at me. Look at me. Come on, you are doing great!!" Before he knew it, he swam all the way across the entire pool! Why? He wasn't looking at the water. He was looking at his dad. He wanted to get to him. He was keeping his eyes on me and he made it through the water. He did something he didn't think he could do.

Lift up your eyes. Get them off the problem. Stop thinking about the problem. If you are thinking about the problem, the struggle, the frustration, the doubt, and the despair—it's just horrible, and terrible, and blackness of night, and you will feel like giving up! Guess what you are going to do? Give up. If your eyes are always on the problem, or the irritation or storm, you will struggle and waver and doubt. Your focus is on the wrong thing! Come on—lift up your eyes!

5. Get some tenacity.

This is what I call "Pit-bull faith." The kind of faith that grabs on and doesn't let go. There was a man whose cattle were being attacked, mauled, and killed by a mountain lion. He had done just about all he could to protect his herd. There were traps and bait, sleepless nights on watch, hunting parties—all to no avail. Finally he got a word of advice from a friend. "Get a Pit-bull," his friend said. "Once they take hold they never let go." Since he had run out of options, the man inquired where he might get one of these dogs. When he came into the owner's barn, he was surprised at the size of the dog. The owner looked at the rancher and smiled. "Yup. He's not big, but it's not the size that gets you. It's that Pit-bull tenacity." The rancher, unsure of the possibilities, bought the dog. After some time of training and work, he staked the dog near the herd one night. The rancher woke to the growl of the dog and believing the mountain lion was nearby, unleashed the pit-bull and off the dog charged into the darkness. What followed was one of the eeriest sounds he had ever heard as somewhere in the night the age-old hatred between cats and dogs was at fever pitch. At daybreak the rancher and a neighbor tracked the blood trail into a canyon. There they found the dog and the mountain lion both dead. The mountain lion was a huge animal that dwarfed the pit-bull. But the dog had clenched its teeth around the throat of that cat and never let go. Its body was clawed and beaten to death, but its grip on its prey held fast. The rancher muttered to himself, "Now that's pit-bull tenacity!"

Scripture tells us that our adversary, the devil, is like a roaring lion, seeking whom he may devour. Our enemy will throw everything at us to overwhelm us and defeat us. Life's circumstances will unload with both barrels and try to destroy our faith. We must get some tenacity in our faith, grab ahold of God's promises and never let go.

Friend, stand strong in your faith! Don't give up! Don't give in! Stand strong in your faith! Let your faith become unswayable, immoveable, and unstoppable. No force on earth, no emotion of the soul, and no demon in hell will overwhelm your faith! Believe in God's Word no matter what life throws at you. Stand strong in faith in spite of every storm.

No famine, no discouragement, no battle, no struggle can extinguish this fire of faith that burns in your heart. When you stand in faith like this—it will transform you. It will give birth to a new future and fulfilled promises. Don't wait. Seize this moment with a grip of faith. Because this is when faith matters most!

Notes

Chapter 3

1. Wendell Smith, *The Roots of Character* (Portland: City Bible Publishing, 1994), chart 2.

Chapter 7

1. John C. Maxwell, *Failing Forward* (Nashville: Thomas Nelson, 2000), 13.

2. Ibid., 13

3. Ibid., 14

4. Ibid., 14

5. Ibid., 15

6. Ibid., 15

7. Ibid., 16

8. Ibid., 16

9. Ibid., 16

10. Ibid., 16-17

11. Ibid., 11

12. Ibid., 26

13. Ibid., 38

14. Ibid., 49

CPSIA information can be obtained at www.ICGtesting.com
Printed in the USA
BVOW071736170112

280767BV00001B/4/P